The Sacred Heart of Jesus

Encyclicals on the Sacred Heart, Prayers of Reparation and Consecration to the Sacred Heart of Jesus

:

DEDICATION

This is dedicated to the Sacred Heart of Jesus.

CONTENTS

PREFACE FOR THE FEAST OF THE SACRED HEART

It is truly meet and just, right and for our salvation, that we should at all times and in all places give thanks to Thee, holy Lord, Father almighty, eternal God: Whose will it was that Thine only-begotten Son, while hanging on the Cross, should be pierced by the soldier's lance, that the Heart thus opened should, as from a well of divine bounty, pour over us streams of mercy and of grace: and that the Heart which never ceased to burn with love for us, should be for the devout a haven of rest and for the penitent an open refuge of salvation.

PREFACE FOR THE FEAST OF THE KINGSHIP OF OUR LORD

It is truly meet and just, right and for our salvation, that we should at all times and in all places give thanks to Thee, holy Lord, Father almighty, eternal God; Who with the oil of gladness didst anoint Thine only-begotten Son our Lord Jesus Christ as Priest for ever and King of all: that by offering Himself on the altar of the Cross, a stainless Victim to appease Thee, He might accomplish the mysteries of man's redemption: and that subjecting all creatures to His sway, He might present to Thine infinite Majesty a universal and eternal Kingdom: a Kingdom of holiness and grace: a Kingdom of justice, love and peace.

ANNUM SACRUM

May 25, 1889

ENCYCLICAL OF POPE LEO XIII
ON CONSECRATION TO THE SACRED HEART

To the Patriarchs, Primates, Archbishops, and Bishops of the Catholic World in Grace and Communion with the Apostolic See.

Venerable Brethren, Health and Apostolic Benediction.

1.But a short time ago, as you well know, We, by letters apostolic, and following the custom and ordinances of Our predecessors, commanded the celebration in this city, at no distant date, of a Holy Year. And now to-day, in the hope and with the object that this religious celebration shall be more devoutly performed, We have traced and recommended a striking design from which, if all shall follow it out with hearty good will, We not unreasonably expect extraordinary and lasting benefits for Christendom in the first place and also for the whole human race.

2. Already more than once We have endeavored, after the example of Our predecessors Innocent XII, Benedict XIII, Clement XIII, Pius VI, and Pius IX., devoutly to foster and bring out into fuller light that most excellent form of devotion which has for its object the veneration of the Sacred Heart of Jesus; this We did especially by the Decree given on June 28, 1889, by which We raised the Feast under that name to the dignity of the first class. But now We have in mind a more signal form of devotion which shall be in a manner the crowning perfection of all the honors that people have been accustomed to pay to the Sacred Heart, and which We confidently trust will be most pleasing to Jesus Christ, our Redeemer. This is not the first time, however, that the design of which We speak has

been mooted. Twenty-five years ago, on the approach of the solemnities of the second centenary of the Blessed Margaret Mary Alacoque's reception of the Divine command to propagate the worship of the Sacred Heart, many letters from all parts, not merely from private persons but from Bishops also were sent to Pius IX begging that he would consent to consecrate the whole human race to the Most Sacred Heart of Jesus. It was thought best at the time to postpone the matter in order that a well-considered decision might be arrived at. Meanwhile permission was granted to individual cities which desired it thus to consecrate themselves, and a form of consecration was drawn up. Now, for certain new and additional reasons, We consider that the plan is ripe for fulfilment.

3. This world-wide and solemn testimony of allegiance and piety is especially appropriate to Jesus Christ, who is the Head and Supreme Lord of the race. His empire extends not only over Catholic nations and those who, having been duly washed in the waters of holy baptism, belong of right to the Church, although erroneous opinions keep them astray, or dissent from her teaching cuts them off from her care; it comprises also all those who are deprived of the Christian faith, so that the whole human race is most truly under the power of Jesus Christ. For He who is the Only-begotten Son of God the Father, having the same substance with Him and being the brightness of His glory and the figure of His substance (Hebrews i., 3) necessarily has everything in common with the Father, and therefore sovereign power over all things. This is why the Son of God thus speaks of Himself through the Prophet: "But I am appointed king by him over Sion, his holy mountain. . . The Lord said to me, Thou art my son, this day have I begotten thee. Ask of me and I will give thee the Gentiles for thy inheritance and the utmost parts of the earth for thy possession" (Psalm, ii.). By these words He declares that He has power from God over the whole Church, which is signified by Mount Sion, and also over the rest of the world to its uttermost ends. On what foundation this sovereign

power rests is made sufficiently plain by the words, "Thou art My Son." For by the very fact that He is the Son of the King of all, He is also the heir of all His Father's power: hence the words-"I will give thee the Gentiles for thy inheritance," which are similar to those used by Paul the Apostle, "whom he bath appointed heir of all things" (Hebrews i., 2).

4. But we should now give most special consideration to the declarations made by Jesus Christ, not through the Apostles or the Prophets but by His own words. To the Roman Governor who asked Him, "Art thou a king then?" He answered unhesitatingly, "Thou sayest that I am a king" (John xviii. 37). And the greatness of this power and the boundlessness of His kingdom is still more clearly declared in these words to the Apostles: "All power is given to me in heaven and on earth" (Matthew xxviii., 18). If then all power has been given to Christ it follows of necessity that His empire must be supreme, absolute and independent of the will of any other, so that none is either equal or like unto it: and since it has been given in heaven and on earth it ought to have heaven and earth obedient to it. And verily he has acted on this extraordinary and peculiar right when He commanded His Apostles to preach His doctrine over the earth, to gather all men together into the one body of the Church by the baptism of salvation, and to bind them by laws, which no one could reject without risking his eternal salvation.

5. But this is not all. Christ reigns not only by natural right as the Son of God, but also by a right that He has acquired. For He it was who snatched us "from the power of darkness" (Colossians i., 13), and "gave Himself for the redemption of all" (I Timothy ii., 6). Therefore not only Catholics, and those who have duly received Christian baptism, but also all men, individually and collectively, have become to Him "a purchased people" (I Peter ii., 9). St. Augustine's words are therefore to the point when he says: "You ask what price He paid? See what He gave and you will understand

how much He paid. The price was the blood of Christ. What could cost so much but the whole world, and all its people? The great price He paid was paid for all" (T. 120 on St. John).

6. How it comes about that infidels themselves are subject to the power and dominion of Jesus Christ is clearly shown by St. Thomas, who gives us the reason and its explanation. For having put the question whether His judicial power extends to all men, and having stated that judicial authority flows naturally from royal authority, he concludes decisively as follows: "All things are subject to Christ as far as His power is concerned, although they are not all subject to Him in the exercise of that power" (3a., p., q. 59, a. 4). This sovereign power of Christ over men is exercised by truth, justice, and above all, by charity.

7. To this twofold ground of His power and domination He graciously allows us, if we think fit, to add voluntary consecration. Jesus Christ, our God and our Redeemer, is rich in the fullest and perfect possession of all things: we, on the other hand, are so poor and needy that we have nothing of our own to offer Him as a gift. But yet, in His infinite goodness and love, He in no way objects to our giving and consecrating to Him what is already His, as if it were really our own; nay, far from refusing such an offering, He positively desires it and asks for it: "My son, give me thy heart." We are, therefore, able to be pleasing to Him by the good will and the affection of our soul. For by consecrating ourselves to Him we not only declare our open and free acknowledgment and acceptance of His authority over us, but we also testify that if what we offer as a gift were really our own, we would still offer it with our whole heart. We also beg of Him that He would vouchsafe to receive it from us, though clearly His own. Such is the efficacy of the act of which We speak, such is the meaning underlying Our words.

8. And since there is in the Sacred Heart a symbol and a sensible image of the infinite love of Jesus Christ which moves us to love one another, therefore is it fit and proper that we should consecrate ourselves to His most Sacred Heart-an act which is nothing else than an offering and a binding of oneself to Jesus Christ, seeing that whatever honor, veneration and love is given to this divine Heart is really and truly given to Christ Himself.

9. For these reasons We urge and exhort all who know and love this divine Heart willingly to undertake this act of piety; and it is Our earnest desire that all should make it on the same day, that so the aspirations of so many thousands who are performing this act of consecration may be borne to the temple of heaven on the same day. But shall We allow to slip from Our remembrance those innumerable others upon whom the light of Christian truth has not yet shined? We hold the place of Him who came to save that which was lost, and who shed His blood for the salvation of the whole human race. And so We greatly desire to bring to the true life those who sit in the shadow of death. As we have already sent messengers of Christ over the earth to instruct them, so now, in pity for their lot with all Our soul we commend them, and as far as in us lies We consecrate them to the Sacred Heart of Jesus. In this way this act of devotion, which We recommend, will be a blessing to all. For having performed it, those in whose hearts are the knowledge and love of Jesus Christ will feel that faith and love increased. Those who knowing Christ, yet neglect His law and its precepts, may still gain from His Sacred Heart the flame of charity. And lastly, for those still more unfortunate, who are struggling in the darkness of superstition, we shall all with one mind implore the assistance of heaven that Jesus Christ, to whose power they are subject, may also one day render them submissive to its exercise; and that not only in the life to come when He will fulfil His will upon all men, by saving some and punishing others, (St. Thomas, ibid), but also in this mortal life by giving them faith and holiness. May they by these

virtues strive to honor God as they ought, and to win everlasting happiness in heaven.

10. Such an act of consecration, since it can establish or draw tighter the bonds which naturally connect public affairs with God, gives to States a hope of better things. In these latter times especially, a policy has been followed which has resulted in a sort of wall being raised between the Church and civil society. In the constitution and administration of States the authority of sacred and divine law is utterly disregarded, with a view to the exclusion of religion from having any constant part in public life. This policy almost tends to the removal of the Christian faith from our midst, and, if that were possible, of the banishment of God Himself from the earth. When men's minds are raised to such a height of insolent pride, what wonder is it that the greater part of the human race should have fallen into such disquiet of mind and be buffeted by waves so rough that no one is suffered to be free from anxiety and peril? When religion is once discarded it follows of necessity that the surest foundations of the public welfare must give way, whilst God, to inflict on His enemies the punishment they so richly deserve, has left them the prey of their own evil desires, so that they give themselves up to their passions and finally wear themselves out by excess of liberty.

11. Hence that abundance of evils which have now for a long time settled upon the world, and which pressingly call upon us to seek for help from Him by whose strength alone they can be driven away. Who can He be but Jesus Christ the Only-begotten Son of God? "For there is no other name under heaven given to men whereby we must be saved" (Acts iv., 12). We must have recourse to Him who is the Way, the Truth and the Life. We have gone astray and we must return to the right path: darkness has overshadowed our minds, and the gloom must be dispelled by the light of truth: death has seized upon us, and we must lay hold of life. It will at

length be possible that our many wounds be healed and all justice spring forth again with the hope of restored authority; that the splendors of peace be renewed, and swords and arms drop from the hand when all men shall acknowledge the empire of Christ and willingly obey His word, and "Every tongue shall confess that our Lord Jesus Christ is in the glory of God the Father" (Philippians ii, II).

12. When the Church, in the days immediately succeeding her institution, was oppressed beneath the yoke of the Caesars, a young Emperor saw in the heavens across, which became at once the happy omen and cause of the glorious victory that soon followed. And now, to-day, behold another blessed and heavenly token is offered to our sight-the most Sacred Heart of Jesus, with a cross rising from it and shining forth with dazzling splendor amidst flames of love. In that Sacred Heart all our hopes should be placed, and from it the salvation of men is to be confidently besought.

13. Finally, there is one motive which We are unwilling to pass over in silence, personal to Ourselves it is true, but still good and weighty, which moves Us to undertake this celebration. God, the author of every good, not long ago preserved Our life by curing Us of a dangerous disease. We now wish, by this increase of the honor paid to the Sacred Heart, that the memory of this great mercy should be brought prominently forward, and Our gratitude be publicly acknowledged.

14. For these reasons, We ordain that on the ninth, tenth and eleventh of the coming month of June, in the principal church of every town and village, certain prayers be said, and on each of these days there be added to the other prayers the Litany of the Sacred Heart approved by Our authority. On the last day the form of consecration shall be recited which, Venerable Brethren, We sent to you with these letters.

15. As a pledge of divine benefits, and in token of Our paternal benevolence, to you, and to the clergy and people committed to your care, We lovingly grant in the Lord the Apostolic Benediction.

Given in Rome at St. Peter's on the 25th day of May, 1899, the twenty-second year of Our Pontificate.

MISERENTISSIMUS REDEMPTOR

May 8, 1928

ENCYCLICAL OF POPE PIUS XI ON REPARATION TO THE
SACRED HEART

Venerable Brethren, Health and the Apostolic Blessing.

Our Most Merciful Redeemer, after He had wrought salvation for
mankind on the tree of the Cross and before He ascended from out
this world to the Father, said to his Apostles and Disciples, to
console them in their anxiety, "Behold I am with you all days, even
to the consummation of the world." (Matt. xxviii, 20). These words,
which are indeed most pleasing, are a cause of all hope and security,
and they bring us, Venerable Brethren, ready succor, whenever we
look round from this watch-tower raised on high and see all human
society laboring amid so many evils and miseries, and the Church
herself beset without ceasing by attacks and machinations. For as
in the beginning this Divine promise lifted up the despondent spirit
of the Apostles and enkindled and inflamed them so that they might
cast the seeds of the Gospel teaching throughout the whole world;
so ever since it has strengthened the Church unto her victory over
the gates of hell. In sooth, Our Lord Jesus Christ has been with his
Church in every age, but He has been with her with more present
aid and protection whenever she has been assailed by graver perils
and difficulties. For the remedies adapted to the condition of time
and circumstances, are always supplied by Divine Wisdom, who
reacheth from end to end mightily, and ordereth all things sweetly
(Wisdom viii, 1). But in this latter age also, "the hand of the Lord is
not shortened" (Isaias lix, 1), more especially since error has crept
in and has spread far and wide, so that it might well be feared that
the fountains of Christian life might be in a manner dried up, where
men are cut off from the love and knowledge of God. Now, since

it may be that some of the people do not know, and others do not heed, those complaints which the most loving Jesus made when He manifested Himself to Margaret Mary Alacoque, and those things likewise which at the same time He asked and expected of men, for their own ultimate profit, it is our pleasure, Venerable Brethren, to speak to you for a little while concerning the duty of honorable satisfaction which we all owe to the Most Sacred Heart of Jesus, with the intent that you may, each of you, carefully teach your own flocks those things which we set before you, and stir them up to put the same in practice.

2. Among the many proofs of the boundless benignity of our Redeemer, there is one that stands out conspicuously, to wit the fact that when the charity of Christian people was growing cold, the Divine Charity itself was set forth to be honored by a special worship, and the riches of its bounty was made widely manifest by that form of devotion wherein worship is given to the Most Sacred Heart of Jesus, "In whom are hid all the treasures of wisdom and knowledge" (Coloss. ii, 3). For as in olden time when mankind came forth from Noe's ark, God set His "bow in the clouds" (Genesis ix, 13), shining as the sign of a friendly covenant; so in the most turbulent times of a more recent age, when the Jansenist heresy, the most crafty of them all, hostile to love and piety towards God, was creeping in and preaching that God was not to be loved as a father but rather to be feared as an implacable judge; then the most benign Jesus showed his own most Sacred Heart to the nations lifted up as a standard of peace and charity portending no doubtful victory in the combat. And indeed Our Predecessor of happy memory, Leo XIII, admiring the timely opportuneness of the devotion to the Most Sacred Heart of Jesus, said very aptly in his Encyclical Letter, "Annum Sacrum," "When in the days near her origin, the Church was oppressed under the yoke of the Caesars the Cross shown on high to the youthful Emperor was at once an omen and a cause of the victory that speedily followed. And here today another most

12

auspicious and most divine sign is offered to our sight, to wit the most Sacred Heart of Jesus, with a Cross set above it shining with most resplendent brightness in the midst of flames. Herein must all hopes be set, from hence must the salvation of men be sought and expected."

3. And rightly indeed is that said, Venerable Brethren. For is not the sum of all religion and therefore the pattern of more perfect life, contained in that most auspicious sign and in the form of piety that follows from it inasmuch as it more readily leads the minds of men to an intimate knowledge of Christ Our Lord, and more efficaciously moves their hearts to love Him more vehemently and to imitate Him more closely? It is no wonder, therefore, that Our Predecessors have constantly defended this most approved form of devotion from the censures of calumniators, and have extolled it with high praise and promoted it very zealously, as the needs of time and circumstance demanded. Moreover, by the inspiration of God's grace, it has come to pass that the pious devotion of the faithful towards the Most Sacred Heart of Jesus has made great increase in the course of time; hence pious confraternities to promote the worship of the Divine Heart are everywhere erected, hence too the custom of receiving Holy Communion on the first Friday of every month at the desire of Christ Jesus, a custom which now prevails everywhere.

4. But assuredly among those things which properly pertain to the worship of the Most Sacred Heart, a special place must be given to that Consecration, whereby we devote ourselves and all things that are ours to the Divine Heart of Jesus, acknowledging that we have received all things from the everlasting love of God. When Our Savior had taught Margaret Mary, the most innocent disciple of His Heart, how much He desired that this duty of devotion should be rendered to him by men, moved in this not so much by His own right as by His immense charity for us; she herself, with her spiritual

father, Claude de la Colombiere, rendered it the first of all. Thereafter followed, in the course of time, individual men, then private families and associations, and lastly civil magistrates, cities and kingdoms. But since in the last century, and in this present century, things have come to such a pass, that by the machinations of wicked men the sovereignty of Christ Our Lord has been denied and war is publicly waged against the Church, by passing laws and promoting plebiscites repugnant to Divine and natural law, nay more by holding assemblies of them that cry out, "We will not have this man to reign over us" (Luke xix, 14): from the aforesaid Consecration there burst forth over against them in keenest opposition the voice of all the clients of the Most Sacred Heart, as it were one voice, to vindicate His glory and to assert His rights: "Christ must reign" (1 Corinthians xv, 25); "Thy kingdom come" (Matth. vi, 10). From this at length it happily came to pass that at the beginning of this century the whole human race which Christ, in whom all things are re-established (Ephes. i, 10), possesses by native right as His own, was dedicated to the same Most Sacred Heart, with the applause of the whole Christian world, by Our Predecessor of happy memory, Leo XIII.

5. Now these things so auspiciously and happily begun as we taught in Our Encyclical Letter "Quas primas," we Ourselves, consenting to very many long-continued desires and prayers of Bishops and people, brought to completion and perfected, by God's grace, when at the close of the Jubilee Year, We instituted the Feast of Christ the King of All, to be solemnly celebrated throughout the whole Christian world. Now when we did this, not only did we set in a clear light that supreme sovereignty which Christ holds over the whole universe, over civil and domestic society, and over individual men, but at the same time we anticipated the joys of that most auspicious day, whereon the whole world will gladly and willingly render obedience to the most sweet lordship of Christ the King. For this reason, We decreed at the same time that this same

Consecration should be renewed every year on the occasion of that appointed festal day, so that the fruit of this same Consecration might be obtained more certainly and more abundantly, and all peoples might be joined together in Christian charity and in the reconciliation of peace, in the Heart of the King of kings and Lord of lords.

6. But to all these duties, more especially to that fruitful Consecration which was in a manner confirmed by the sacred solemnity of Christ the King, something else must needs be added, and it is concerning this that it is our pleasure to speak with you more at length, Venerable Brethren, on the present occasion: we mean that duty of honorable satisfaction or reparation which must be rendered to the Most Sacred Heart of Jesus. For if the first and foremost thing in Consecration is this, that the creature's love should be given in return for the love of the Creator, another thing follows from this at once, namely that to the same uncreated Love, if so be it has been neglected by forgetfulness or violated by offense, some sort of compensation must be rendered for the injury, and this debt is commonly called by the name of reparation.

7. Now though in both these matters we are impelled by quite the same motives, none the less we are holden to the duty of reparation and expiation by a certain more valid title of justice and of love, of justice indeed, in order that the offense offered to God by our sins may be expiated and that the violated order may be repaired by penance: and of love too so that we may suffer together with Christ suffering and "filled with reproaches" (Lam. iii, 30), and for all our poverty may offer Him some little solace. For since we are all sinners and laden with many faults, our God must be honored by us not only by that worship wherewith we adore His infinite Majesty with due homage, or acknowledge His supreme dominion by praying, or praise His boundless bounty by thanksgiving; but besides this we must need make satisfaction to God the just

avenger, "for our numberless sins and offenses and negligences." To Consecration, therefore, whereby we are devoted to God and are called holy to God, by that holiness and stability which, as the Angelic Doctor teaches, is proper to consecration (2da. 2dae. qu. 81, a. 8. c.), there must be added expiation, whereby sins are wholly blotted out, lest the holiness of the supreme justice may punish our shameless unworthiness, and reject our offering as hateful rather than accept it as pleasing.

8. Moreover this duty of expiation is laid upon the whole race of men since, as we are taught by the Christian faith, after Adam's miserable fall, infected by hereditary stain, subject to concupiscences and most wretchedly depraved, it would have been thrust down into eternal destruction. This indeed is denied by the wise men of this age of ours, who following the ancient error of Pelagius, ascribe to human nature a certain native virtue by which of its own force it can go onward to higher things; but the Apostle rejects these false opinions of human pride, admonishing us that we "were by nature children of wrath" (Ephesians ii, 3). And indeed, even from the beginning, men in a manner acknowledged this common debt of expiation and, led by a certain natural instinct, they endeavored to appease God by public sacrifices.

9. But no created power was sufficient to expiate the sins of men, if the Son of God had not assumed man's nature in order to redeem it. This, indeed, the Savior of men Himself declared by the mouth of the sacred Psalmist: "Sacrifice and oblation thou wouldest not: but a body thou hast fitted to me: Holocausts for sin did not please thee: then said I: Behold I come" (Hebrews x, 5-7). And in very deed, "Surely He hath borne our infirmities, and carried our sorrows. . . He was wounded for our iniquities (Isaias liii, 4-5), and He His own self bore our sins in His body upon the tree . . . (1 Peter ii, 24), "Blotting out the handwriting of the decree that was against us, which was contrary to us. And He has taken the same out of the

way, fastening it to the cross . . ." (Colossians ii, 14) "that we being dead to sins, should live to justice" (1 Peter ii, 24). Yet, though the copious redemption of Christ has abundantly forgiven us all offenses (Cf. Colossians ii, 13), nevertheless, because of that wondrous divine dispensation whereby those things that are wanting of the sufferings of Christ are to be filled up in our flesh for His body which is the Church (Cf. Colossians i, 24), to the praises and satisfactions, "which Christ in the name of sinners rendered unto God" we can also add our praises and satisfactions, and indeed it behoves us so to do. But we must ever remember that the whole virtue of the expiation depends on the one bloody sacrifice of Christ, which without intermission of time is renewed on our altars in an unbloody manner, "For the victim is one and the same, the same now offering by the ministry of priests, who then offered Himself on the cross, the manner alone of offering being different" (Council of Trent, Session XXIII, Chapter 2). Wherefore with this most august Eucharistic Sacrifice there ought to be joined an oblation both of the ministers and of all the faithful, so that they also may "present themselves living sacrifices, holy, pleasing unto God" (Romans xii, 1). Nay more, St. Cyprian does not hesitate to affirm that "the Lord's sacrifice is not celebrated with legitimate sanctification, unless our oblation and sacrifice correspond to His passion" (Ephesians 63). For this reason, the Apostle admonishes us that "bearing about in our body the mortification of Jesus" (2 Corinthians iv, 10), and buried together with Christ, and planted together in the likeness of His death (Cf. Romans vi, 4-5), we must not only crucify our flesh with the vices and concupiscences (Cf. Galatians v, 24), "flying the corruption of that concupiscence which is in the world" (2 Peter i, 4), but "that the life also of Jesus may be made manifest in our bodies" (2 Corinthians iv, 10) and being made partakers of His eternal priesthood we are to offer up "gifts and sacrifices for sins" (Hebrews v, 1). Nor do those only enjoy a participation in this mystic priesthood and in the office of satisfying and sacrificing, whom our Pontiff Christ Jesus uses as His ministers to offer up the clean oblation to God's Name in every place from the rising of the sun to the going down (Malachias i, 11), but the whole Christian people rightly called by the Prince of the Apostles "a chosen generation, a kingly priesthood" (1 Peter ii, 9), ought to offer for sins both for itself and for all mankind (Cf. Hebrews v, 3), in much the same manner as every priest and pontiff "taken from among men, is ordained for men in the things that appertain to God" (Hebrews v, 1).

10. But the more perfectly that our oblation and sacrifice corresponds to the sacrifice of Our Lord, that is to say, the more perfectly we have immolated our love and our desires and have crucified our flesh by that mystic crucifixion of which the Apostle speaks, the more abundant fruits of that propitiation and expiation shall we receive for ourselves and for others. For there is a wondrous and close union of all the faithful with Christ, such as that which prevails between the head and the other members; moreover by that mystic Communion of Saints which we profess in the Catholic creed, both individual men and peoples are joined together not only with one another but also with him, "who is the head, Christ; from whom the whole body, being compacted and fitly joined together, by what every joint supplieth, according to the operation in the measure of every part, maketh increase of the body unto the edifying of itself in charity" (Ephesians iv, 15-16). It was this indeed that the Mediator of God and men, Christ Jesus, when He was near to death, asked of His Father: "I in them, and thou in me: that they may be made perfect in one" (John xvii, 23).

11. Wherefore, even as consecration proclaims and confirms this union with Christ, so does expiation begin that same union by washing away faults, and perfect it by participating in the sufferings of Christ, and consummate it by offering victims for the brethren. And this indeed was the purpose of the merciful Jesus, when He showed His Heart to us bearing about it the symbols of the passion

and displaying the flames of love, that from the one we might know the infinite malice of sin, and in the other we might admire the infinite charity of Our Redeemer, and so might have a more vehement hatred of sin, and make a more ardent return of love for His love.

12. And truly the spirit of expiation or reparation has always had the first and foremost place in the worship given to the Most Sacred Heart of Jesus, and nothing is more in keeping with the origin, the character, the power, and the distinctive practices of this form of devotion, as appears from the record of history and custom, as well as from the sacred liturgy and the acts of the Sovereign Pontiffs. For when Christ manifested Himself to Margaret Mary, and declared to her the infinitude of His love, at the same time, in the manner of a mourner, He complained that so many and such great injuries were done to Him by ungrateful men - and we would that these words in which He made this complaint were fixed in the minds of the faithful, and were never blotted out by oblivion: "Behold this Heart" - He said - "which has loved men so much and has loaded them with all benefits, and for this boundless love has had no return but neglect, and contumely, and this often from those who were bound by a debt and duty of a more special love." In order that these faults might be washed away, He then recommended several things to be done, and in particular the following as most pleasing to Himself, namely that men should approach the Altar with this purpose of expiating sin, making what is called a Communion of Reparation, - and that they should likewise make expiatory supplications and prayers, prolonged for a whole hour, - which is rightly called the "Holy Hour." These pious exercises have been approved by the Church and have also been enriched with copious indulgences.

13. But how can these rites of expiation bring solace now, when Christ is already reigning in the beatitude of Heaven? To this we

may answer in some words of St. Augustine which are very apposite here, - "Give me one who loves, and he will understand what I say" (In Johannis evangelium, tract. XXVI, 4). For any one who has great love of God, if he will look back through the tract of past time may dwell in meditation on Christ, and see Him laboring for man, sorrowing, suffering the greatest hardships, "for us men and for our salvation," well-nigh worn out with sadness, with anguish, nay "bruised for our sins" (Isaias liii, 5), and healing us by His bruises. And the minds of the pious meditate on all these things the more truly, because the sins of men and their crimes committed in every age were the cause why Christ was delivered up to death, and now also they would of themselves bring death to Christ, joined with the same griefs and sorrows, since each several sin in its own way is held to renew the passion of Our Lord: "Crucifying again to themselves the Son of God, and making him a mockery" (Hebrews vi, 6). Now if, because of our sins also which were as yet in the future, but were foreseen, the soul of Christ became sorrowful unto death, it cannot be doubted that then, too, already He derived somewhat of solace from our reparation, which was likewise foreseen, when "there appeared to Him an angel from heaven" (Luke xxii, 43), in order that His Heart, oppressed with weariness and anguish, might find consolation. And so even now, in a wondrous yet true manner, we can and ought to console that Most Sacred Heart which is continually wounded by the sins of thankless men, since - as we also read in the sacred liturgy - Christ Himself, by the mouth of the Psalmist complains that He is forsaken by His friends: "My Heart hath expected reproach and misery, and I looked for one that would grieve together with me, but there was none: and for one that would comfort me, and I found none" (Psalm lxviii, 21).

14. To this it may be added that the expiatory passion of Christ is renewed and in a manner continued and fulfilled in His mystical body, which is the Church. For, to use once more the words of St.

Augustine, "Christ suffered whatever it behoved Him to suffer; now nothing is wanting of the measure of the sufferings. Therefore the sufferings were fulfilled, but in the head; there were yet remaining the sufferings of Christ in His body" (In Psalm lxxxvi). This, indeed, Our Lord Jesus Himself vouchsafed to explain when, speaking to Saul, "as yet breathing out threatenings and slaughter" (Acts ix, 1), He said, "I am Jesus whom thou persecutest" (Acts ix, 5), clearly signifying that when persecutions are stirred up against the Church, the Divine Head of the Church is Himself attacked and troubled. Rightly, therefore, does Christ, still suffering in His mystical body, desire to have us partakers of His expiation, and this is also demanded by our intimate union with Him, for since we are "the body of Christ and members of member" (1 Corinthians xii, 27), whatever the head suffers, all the members must suffer with it (Cf. 1 Corinthians xii, 26).

15. Now, how great is the necessity of this expiation or reparation, more especially in this our age, will be manifest to every one who, as we said at the outset, will examine the world, "seated in wickedness" (1 John v, 19), with his eyes and with his mind. For from all sides the cry of the peoples who are mourning comes up to us, and their princes or rulers have indeed stood up and met together in one against the Lord and against His Church (Cf. Psalm ii, 2). Throughout those regions indeed, we see that all rights both human and Divine are confounded. Churches are thrown down and overturned, religious men and sacred virgins are torn from their homes and are afflicted with abuse, with barbarities, with hunger and imprisonment; bands of boys and girls are snatched from the bosom of their mother the Church, and are induced to renounce Christ, to blaspheme and to attempt the worst crimes of lust; the whole Christian people, sadly disheartened and disrupted, are continually in danger of falling away from the faith, or of suffering the most cruel death. These things in truth are so sad that you might say that such events foreshadow and portend the "beginning of

sorrows," that is to say of those that shall be brought by the man of sin, "who is lifted up above all that is called God or is worshipped" (2 Thessalonians ii, 4).

16. But it is yet more to be lamented, Venerable Brethren, that among the faithful themselves, washed in Baptism with the blood of the immaculate Lamb, and enriched with grace, there are found so many men of every class, who laboring under an incredible ignorance of Divine things and infected with false doctrines, far from their Father's home, lead a life involved in vices, a life which is not brightened by the light of true faith, nor gladdened by the hope of future beatitude, nor refreshed and cherished by the fire of charity; so that they truly seem to sit in darkness and in the shadow of death. Moreover, among the faithful there is a greatly increasing carelessness of ecclesiastical discipline, and of those ancient institutions on which all Christian life rests, by which domestic society is governed, and the sanctity of marriage is safeguarded; the education of children is altogether neglected, or else it is depraved by too indulgent blandishments, and the Church is even robbed of the power of giving the young a Christian education; there is a sad forgetfulness of Christian modesty especially in the life and the dress of women; there is an unbridled cupidity of transitory things, a want of moderation in civic affairs, an unbounded ambition of popular favor, a depreciation of legitimate authority, and lastly a contempt for the word of God, whereby faith itself is injured, or is brought into proximate peril.

17. But all these evils as it were culminate in the cowardice and the sloth of those who, after the manner of the sleeping and fleeing disciples, wavering in their faith, miserably forsake Christ when He is oppressed by anguish or surrounded by the satellites of Satan, and in the perfidy of those others who following the example of the traitor Judas, either partake of the holy table rashly and sacrilegiously, or go over to the camp of the enemy. And thus, even

against our will, the thought rises in the mind that now those days draw near of which Our Lord prophesied: "And because iniquity hath abounded, the charity of many shall grow cold" (Matth. xxiv, 12).

18. Now, whosoever of the faithful have piously pondered on all these things must need be inflamed with the charity of Christ in His agony and make a more vehement endeavor to expiate their own faults and those of others, to repair the honor of Christ, and to promote the eternal salvation of souls. And indeed that saying of the Apostle: "Where sin abounded, grace did more abound" (Romans v, 20) may be used in a manner to describe this present age; for while the wickedness of men has been greatly increased, at the same time, by the inspiration of the Holy Ghost, a marvelous increase has been made in the number of the faithful of both sexes who with eager mind endeavor to make satisfaction for the many injuries offered to the Divine Heart, nay more they do not hesitate to offer themselves to Christ as victims. For indeed if any one will lovingly dwell on those things of which we have been speaking, and will have them deeply fixed in his mind, it cannot be but he will shrink with horror from all sin as from the greatest evil, and more than this he will yield himself wholly to the will of God, and will strive to repair the injured honor of the Divine Majesty, as well by constantly praying, as by voluntary mortifications, by patiently bearing the afflictions that befall him, and lastly by spending his whole life in this exercise of expiation.

19. And for this reason also there have been established many religious families of men and women whose purpose it is by earnest service, both by day and by night, in some manner to fulfill the office of the Angel consoling Jesus in the garden; hence come certain associations of pious men, approved by the Apostolic See and enriched with indulgences, who take upon themselves this same duty of making expiation, a duty which is to be fulfilled by

fitting exercises of devotion and of the virtues; hence lastly, to omit other things, come the devotions and solemn demonstrations for the purpose of making reparation to the offended Divine honor, which are inaugurated everywhere, not only by pious members of the faithful, but by parishes, dioceses and cities.

20. These things being so, Venerable Brethren, just as the rite of consecration, starting from humble beginnings, and afterwards more widely propagated, was at length crowned with success by Our confirmation; so in like manner, we earnestly desire that this custom of expiation or pious reparation, long since devoutly introduced and devoutly propagated, may also be more firmly sanctioned by Our Apostolic authority and more solemnly celebrated by the whole Catholic name. Wherefore, we decree and command that every year on the Feast of the Most Sacred Heart of Jesus, - which feast indeed on this occasion we have ordered to be raised to the degree of a double of the first class with an octave - in all churches throughout the whole world, the same expiatory prayer or protestation as it is called, to Our most loving Savior, set forth in the same words according to the copy subjoined to this letter shall be solemnly recited, so that all our faults may be washed away with tears, and reparation may be made for the violated rights of Christ the supreme King and Our most loving Lord.

21. There is surely no reason for doubting, Venerable Brethren, that from this devotion piously established and commanded to the whole Church, many excellent benefits will flow forth not only to individual men but also to society, sacred, civil, and domestic, seeing that our Redeemer Himself promised to Margaret Mary that "all those who rendered this honor to His Heart would be endowed with an abundance of heavenly graces." Sinners indeed, looking on Him whom they pierced (John xix, 37), moved by the sighs and tears of the whole Church, by grieving for the injuries offered to the supreme King, will return to the heart (Isaias xlvi, 8), lest

perchance being hardened in their faults, when they see Him whom they pierced "coming in the clouds of heaven" (Matth. xxvi, 64), too late and in vain they shall bewail themselves because of Him (Cf. Apoc. i, 7). But the just shall be justified and shall be sanctified still (Cf. Apoc. xxii. 11) and they will devote themselves wholly and with new ardor to the service of their King, when they see Him contemned and attacked and assailed with so many and such great insults, but more than all will they burn with zeal for the eternal salvation of souls when they have pondered on the complaint of the Divine Victim: "What profit is there in my blood?" (Psalm xxix, 10), and likewise on the joy that will be felt by the same Most Sacred Heart of Jesus "upon one sinner doing penance" (Luke xv, 10). And this indeed we more especially and vehemently desire and confidently expect, that the just and merciful God who would have spared Sodom for the sake of ten just men, will much more be ready to spare the whole race of men, when He is moved by the humble petitions and happily appeased by the prayers of the community of the faithful praying together in union with Christ their Mediator and Head, in the name of all. And now lastly may the most benign Virgin Mother of God smile on this purpose and on these desires of ours; for since she brought forth for us Jesus our Redeemer, and nourished Him, and offered Him as a victim by the Cross, by her mystic union with Christ and His very special grace she likewise became and is piously called a reparatress. Trusting in her intercession with Christ, who whereas He is the "one mediator of God and men" (1 Timothy ii, 5), chose to make His Mother the advocate of sinners, and the minister and mediatress of grace, as an earnest of heavenly gifts and as a token of Our paternal affection we most lovingly impart the Apostolic Blessing to you, Venerable Brethren, and to all the flock committed to your care.

Given at Rome, at St. Peter's, on the eighth day of May, 1928, in the seventh year of Our Pontificate.

HAURIETIS AQUAS

May 15, 1956

ENCYCLICAL OF POPE PIUS XII
ON DEVOTION TO THE SACRED HEART

Venerable Brethren: Health and Apostolic Benediction.

1. "You shall draw waters with joy out of the Savior's fountain."(Is. 12:3) These words by which the prophet Isaias, using highly significant imagery, foretold the manifold and abundant gifts of God which the Christian era was to bring forth, come naturally to Our mind when We reflect on the centenary of that year when Our predecessor of immortal memory, Pius IX, gladly yielding to the prayers from the whole Catholic world, ordered the celebration of the feast of the Most Sacred Heart of Jesus in the Universal Church.

2. It is altogether impossible to enumerate the heavenly gifts which devotion to the Sacred Heart of Jesus has poured out on the souls of the faithful, purifying them, offering them heavenly strength, rousing them to the attainment of all virtues. Therefore, recalling those wise words of the Apostle St. James, "Every best gift and every perfect gift is from above, coming down from the Father of Lights,"(Jas. 1:17) We are perfectly justified in seeing in this same devotion, which flourishes with increasing fervor throughout the world, a gift without price which our divine Savior the Incarnate Word, as the one Mediator of grace and truth between the heavenly Father and the human race imparted to the Church, His mystical Spouse, in recent centuries when she had to endure such trials and surmount so many difficulties.

3. The Church, rejoicing in this inestimable gift, can show forth a more ardent love of her divine Founder, and can, in a more generous and effective manner, respond to that invitation which St. John the Evangelist relates as having come from Christ Himself: "And on the last and great day of the festivity, Jesus stood and cried out, saying, 'If

any man thirst, let him come to Me, and let him drink that believeth in Me. As the Scripture saith: Out of his heart there shall flow rivers of living waters.' Now this He said of the Spirit which they should receive who believed in Him."(3)

4. For those who were listening to Jesus speaking, it certainly was not difficult to relate these words by which He promised the fountain of "living water" destined to spring from His own side, to the words of sacred prophecy of Isaias, Ezechiel and Zacharias, foretelling the Messianic Kingdom, and likewise to the symbolic rock from which, when struck by Moses, water flowed forth in a miraculous manner.(4)

5. Divine Love first takes its origin from the Holy Spirit, Who is the Love in Person of the Father and the Son in the bosom of the most Holy Trinity. Most aptly then does the Apostle of the Gentiles echo, as it were, the words of Jesus Christ, when he ascribes the pouring forth of love in the hearts of believers to this Spirit of Love: "The charity of God is poured forth in our hearts by the Holy Spirit Who is given to us."(5)

6. Holy Writ declares that between divine charity, which must burn in the souls of Christians, and the Holy Spirit, Who is certainly Love Itself, there exists the closest bond, which clearly shows all of us, venerable brethren, the intimate nature of that worship which must be paid to the Most Sacred Heart of Jesus Christ. If we consider its special nature it is beyond question that this devotion is an act of religion of high order; it demands of us a complete and unreserved determination to devote and consecrate ourselves to the love of the divine Redeemer, Whose wounded Heart is its living token and symbol. It is equally clear, but at a higher level, that this same devotion provides us with a most powerful means of repaying the divine Lord by our own.

7. Indeed it follows that it is only under the impulse of love that the minds of men obey fully and perfectly the rule of the Supreme Being, since the influence of our love draws us close to the divine Will that it

becomes as it were completely one with it, according to the saying, "He who is joined to the Lord, is one spirit."(6)

8. The Church has always valued, and still does, the devotion to the Most Sacred Heart of Jesus so highly that she provides for the spread of it among Christian peoples everywhere and by every means. At the same time she uses every effort to protect it against the charges of so-called "naturalism" and "sentimentalism." In spite of this it is much to be regretted that, both in the past and in our own times, this most noble devotion does not find a place of honor and esteem among certain Christians and even occasionally not among those who profess themselves moved by zeal for the Catholic religion and the attainment of holiness.

9. "If you but knew the gift of God."(7) With these words, venerable brethren, We who in the secret designs of God have been elected as the guardians and stewards of the sacred treasures of faith and piety which the divine Redeemer has entrusted to His Church, prompted by Our sense of duty, admonish them all.

10. For even though the devotion to the Sacred Heart of Jesus has triumphed so to speak, over the errors and the neglect of men, and has penetrated entirely His Mystical Body; still there are some of Our children who, led astray by prejudices, sometimes go so far as to consider this devotion ill-adapted, not to say detrimental, to the more pressing spiritual needs of the Church and humanity in this present age. There are some who, confusing and confounding the primary nature of this devotion with various individual forms of piety which the Church approves and encourages but does not command, regard this as a kind of additional practice which each one may take up or not according to his own inclination.

11. There are others who reckon this same devotion burdensome and of little or no use to men who are fighting in the army of the divine King and who are inspired mainly by the thought of laboring with their

own strength, their own resources and expenditures of their own time, to defend Catholic truth, to teach and spread it, to instill Christian social teachings, to promote those acts of religion and those undertakings which they consider much more necessary today.

12. Again, there are those who so far from considering this devotion a strong support for the right ordering and renewal of Christian morals both in the individual's private life and in the home circle, see it rather a type of piety nourished not by the soul and mind but by the senses and consequently more suited to the use of women, since it seems to them something not quite suitable for educated men.

13. Moreover there are those who consider a devotion of this kind as primarily demanding penance, expiation and the other virtues which they call "passive," meaning thereby that they produce no external results. Hence they do not think it suitable to re-enkindle the spirit of piety in modern times. Rather, this should aim at open and vigorous action, at the triumph of the Catholic faith, at a strong defense of Christian morals. Christian morality today, as everyone knows, is easily contaminated by the sophistries of those who are indifferent to any form of religion, and who, discarding all distinctions between truth and falsehood, whether in thought or in practice, accept even the most ignoble corruptions of materialistic atheism, or as they call it, secularism.

14. Who does not see, venerable brethren, that opinions of this kind are in entire disagreement with the teachings which Our predecessors officially proclaimed from this seat of truth when approving the devotion to the Sacred Heart of Jesus.? Who would be so bold as to call that devotion useless and inappropriate to our age which Our predecessor of immortal memory, Leo XIII, declared to be "the most acceptable form of piety?" He had no doubt that in it there was a

powerful remedy for the healing of those very evils which today also, and beyond question in a wider and more serious way, bring distress and disquiet to individuals and to the whole human race. "This devotion," he said, "which We recommend to all, will be profitable to all." And he added this counsel and encouragement with reference to the devotion to the Sacred Heart of Jesus: ". . .hence those forces of evil which have now for so long a time been taking root and which so fiercely compel us to seek help from Him by Whose strength alone they can be driven away. Who can He be but Jesus Christ, the only begotten Son of God? 'For there is no other name under heaven given to men whereby we must be saved.'(8) We must have recourse to Him Who is the Way, the Truth, and the Life."(9)

15. No less to be approved, no less suitable for the fostering of Christian piety was this devotion declared to be by Our predecessor of happy memory, Pius XI. In an encyclical letter he wrote: "Is not a summary of all our religion and, moreover, a guide to a more perfect life contained in this one devotion? Indeed, it more easily leads our minds to know Christ the Lord intimately and more effectively turns our hearts to love Him more ardently and to imitate Him more perfectly."(10)

16. To Us, no less than to Our predecessors, these capital truths are clear and certain. When We took up Our office of Supreme Pontiff and saw, in full accord with Our prayers and desires, that the devotion to the Sacred Heart of Jesus had increased and was actually, so to speak, making triumphal progress among Christian peoples, We rejoiced that from it were flowing through the whole Church innumerable and salutary results. This We were pleased to point out in Our first encyclical letter.(11)

17. Through the years of Our pontificate--years filled not only with bitter hardships but also with ineffable consolations these effects have not diminished in number or power or beauty, but on the contrary have increased. Indeed, happily there has begun a variety of projects which are conducive to a rekindling of this devotion. We refer to the formation of cultural associations for the advancement of religion and

of charitable works; publications setting forth the true historical, ascetical and mystical doctrine concerning this entire subject; pious works of atonement; and in particular those manifestations of most ardent piety which the Apostleship of Prayer has brought about, under whose auspices and direction local gatherings - families, colleges, institutions - and sometimes nations have been consecrated to the Sacred Heart of Jesus. To all these We have offered paternal congratulations on many occasions, whether in letters written on the subject, in personal addresses, or even in messages delivered over the radio.(12)

18. Therefore when We perceive so fruitful an abundance of healing waters, that is, heavenly gifts of divine love, issuing from the Sacred Heart of our Redeemer, spreading among countless children of the Catholic Church by the inspiration and action of the divine Spirit; We can only exhort you, venerable brethren, with fatherly affection to join Us in giving tribute of praise and heartfelt thanks to God, the Giver of all good gifts. We make Our own these words of the Apostle of the Gentiles: "Now to Him Who is able to do all things more abundantly than we desire or understand, according to the power that worketh in us, to Him be glory in the Church and in Christ Jesus unto all generations world without end. Amen."(13)

19. But after We have paid Our debt of thanks to the Eternal God, We wish to urge on you and on all Our beloved children of the Church a more earnest consideration of those principles which take their origin from Scripture and the teaching of the Fathers and theologians and on which, as on solid foundations, the worship of the Sacred Heart of Jesus rests. We are absolutely convinced that not until we have made a profound study of the primary and loftier nature of this devotion with the aid of the light of the divinely revealed truth, can we rightly and fully appreciate its incomparable excellence and the inexhaustible abundance of its heavenly favors. Likewise by devout meditation and contemplation of the innumerable benefits produced from it, we will be able to celebrate worthily the completion of the first hundred years

since the observance of the feast of the Sacred Heart of Jesus was extended to the Universal Church.

20. Moved therefore by this consideration, to the end that the minds of the faithful may have from Our hands salutary food and consequently after such nourishment be able more easily to arrive at a deeper understanding of the true nature of this devotion and possess its rich fruits, We will undertake to explain those pages of the Old and New Testament in which the infinite love of God for the human race (which we shall never be able adequately to contemplate) is revealed and set before us. Then, as occasion offers, We shall touch upon the main lines of the commentaries which the Fathers and Doctors of the Church have handed down to us. And finally, We shall strive to set in its true light the very close connection which exists between the form of devotion paid to the Heart of the divine Redeemer and the worship we owe to His love and to the love of the Most Holy Trinity for all men. For We think if only the main elements on which the most excellent form of devotion rests are clarified in the light of Sacred Scripture and the teachings of tradition, Christians can more easily "draw waters with joy out of the Savior's fountains."(14) By this We mean they can appreciate more fully the full weight of the special importance which devotion to the Sacred Heart of Jesus enjoys in the liturgy of the Church and in its internal and external life and action, and can also gather those fruits of salvation by which each one can bring about a healthy reform in his own conduct, as the bishops of the Christian flock desire.

21. That all may understand more exactly the teachings which the selected texts of the Old and New Testament furnish concerning this devotion, they must clearly understand the reasons why the Church gives the highest form of worship to the Heart of the divine Redeemer. As you well know, venerable brethren, the reasons are two in number. The first, which applies also to the other sacred members of the Body of Jesus Christ, rests on that principle whereby we recognize that His Heart, the noblest part of human nature, is hypostatically united to the

Person of the divine Word. Consequently, there must be paid to it that worship of adoration with which the Church honors the Person of the Incarnate Son of God Himself. We are dealing here with an article of faith, for it has been solemnly defined in the general Council of Ephesus and the second Council of Constantinople.(15)

22. The other reason which refers in a particular manner to the Heart of the divine Redeemer, and likewise demands in a special way that the highest form of worship be paid to it, arises from the fact that His Heart, more than all the other members of His body, is the natural sign and symbol of His boundless love for the human race. "There is in the Sacred Heart," as Our predecessor of immortal memory, Leo XIII, pointed out, "the symbol and express image of the infinite love of Jesus Christ which moves us to love in return."(16)

23. It is of course beyond doubt that the Sacred Books never make express mention of a special worship of veneration and love made to the physical Heart of the Incarnate Word as the symbol of His burning love. But if this must certainly be admitted, it cannot cause us surprise nor in any way lead us to doubt the divine love for us which is the principal object of this devotion; since that love is proclaimed and insisted upon in the Old and in the New Testament by the kind of images which strongly arouse our emotions. Since these images were presented in the Sacred Writings foretelling the coming of the Son of God made man, they can be considered as a token of the noblest symbol and witness of that divine love, that is, of the most Sacred and Adorable Heart of the divine Redeemer.

24. We do not think it essential to Our subject to cite at length passages from the Old Testament books which contain truths divinely revealed in ancient times. We consider it sufficient to call to mind that the covenant made between God and the people and sanctified by peace offerings - the first Law of which was written on two tablets and made known by Moses (17) and explained by the prophets -was an agreement established not only on the strong foundation of God's

supreme dominion and of man's duty of obedience but was also based and nourished on more noble considerations of love. The ultimate reason for obeying God, for the people of Israel, was not the fear of divine vengeance which the rumble of thunder and the lightning flashing from the top of Mount Sinai struck into their souls, but was rather the love they owed to God. "Hear, O Israel! The Lord our God is one Lord. Thou shalt love the Lord, thy God, with thy whole heart, and thy whole soul, and thy whole strength. And these words which I command thee this day shall be in thy heart."(18)

25. We do not wonder then, that Moses and the prophets, whom the Angelic Doctor rightly names the "elders" of the chosen people,(19) perceived clearly that the foundation of the whole Law lay on this commandment of love, and described all the circumstances and relationships which should exist between God and His people by metaphors drawn from the natural love of a father and his children, or a man and his wife, rather than from the harsh imagery derived from the supreme dominion of God or the obligation of subjecting ourselves in fear. And so, to take an example, when Moses himself was singing his famous hymn in honor of the people restored to freedom from the slavery of Egypt, and wished to indicate it had come about by the power of God; he used these symbolic and touching expressions: "As the eagle enticing her young to fly, and hovering over them, (God) spread his wings, and hath taken him (Israel) and carried him on his shoulders."(20)

26. But perhaps none of the holy prophets has expressed and revealed as clearly and vividly as Osee the love with which God always watches over His people. In writings of this prophet, who is outstanding among the minor prophets for the sublimity of his concise language, God declares that His love for the chosen people, combining justice and a holy anxiety, is like the love of a merciful and loving father or of a husband whose honor is offended. This love is not diminished or withdrawn in the face of the perfidy or the horrible crimes of those who betray it. If it inflicts just chastisements on the guilty, it is not for

the purpose of rejecting them or of abandoning them to themselves; but rather to bring about the repentance and the purification of the unfaithful spouse and ungrateful children, and to bind them once more to itself with renewed and yet stronger bonds of love. "Because Israel was a child, and I loved him; and I called my son out of Egypt. . .And I was like a foster father to Ephraim, and I carried them in my arms, and they knew not that I healed them. I will draw them with the cords of Adam, with the bonds of love. . .I will heal their wounds, I will love them; for My wrath is turned away from them. I will be as a dew, Israel shall spring up as a lily, and his root shall shoot forth as that of Libanus."(21)

27. Similar sentiments are uttered by the prophet Isaias when he introduces a conversation in the form of question and answer, as it were, between God and the chosen people: "And Sion said, 'the Lord hath forsaken me; the Lord hath forgotten me.' Can a woman forget her infant so as not to have pity on the son of her womb? And if she should forget, yet will not I forget thee."(22)

28. No less moving are the words which the author of the Canticle of Canticles, employing comparisons from conjugal affection, describes symbolically the bonds of mutual love by which God and his chosen people are united to each other: "As the lily among thorns, so is My love among the daughters. . .I to My beloved and My beloved to Me, who feedeth among the lilies. . .Put Me as a seal upon thy heart, as a seal upon thy arm; for love is strong as death, jealousy is hard as hell, the lamps thereof are lamps of fire and flames."(23)

29. This most tender, forgiving and patient love of God, though it deems unworthy the people of Israel as they add sin to sin, nevertheless at no time casts them off entirely. And though it seems strong and exalted indeed, yet it was only an advance symbol of that burning charity which mankind' s promised Redeemer, from His most loving Heart, was destined to open to all and which was to be the type of His love for us and the foundation of the new covenant.

30. Assuredly, when He who is the only begotten of the Father and the Word made flesh "full of grace and truth"(24) had come to men weighed down with many sins and miseries it was He alone, from that human nature united hypostatically to the divine Person, Who could open to the human race the "fountain of living water" which would irrigate the parched land and transform it into a fruitful and flourishing garden.

31. That this most wondrous effect would come to pass as a result of the merciful and everlasting love of God the prophet Jeremias seems to foretell in a manner in these words: "I have loved thee with an everlasting love, therefore I have drawn thee taking pity on thee. . .Behold the days shall come, saith the Lord, and I shall make a new covenant with the house of Israel and with the house of Juda. . .this will be the covenant that I will make with the house of Israel, after those days, saith the Lord; I will give My law in their bowels, and will write it in their heart, and I will be their God and they shall be My people. . .for I will forgive their iniquity and I will remember their sin no more."(25)

32. But it is only in the Gospels that we find definitely and clearly set out the new covenant between God and man; for that covenant which Moses had made between the people of Israel and God was a mere symbol and a sign of the covenant foretold by the prophet Jeremias. We say that this new covenant is that very thing which was established and effected by the work of the Incarnate Word Who is the source of divine grace. This covenant is therefore to be considered incomparably more excellent and more solid because it was ratified, not as in the past by the blood of goats and calves, but by the most precious Blood of Him Whom these same innocent animals, devoid of reason, had already prefigured: "The Lamb of God, who taketh away the sins of the world."(26)

33. The Christian covenant, much more than that of the old, clearly appears as an agreement based not on slavery or on fear, but as one ratified by that friendship which ought to exist between a father and his children, as one nourished and strengthened by a more generous outpouring of divine grace and truth according to the saying of St. John the Evangelist: "And of his fulness we have all received, and grace for grace. For the Law was given by Moses; grace and truth came by Jesus Christ."(27)

34. Since we have been introduced, venerable brethren, to the innermost mystery of the infinite charity of the Word Incarnate by these words of the disciple "whom Jesus loved and who also leaned on His breast at the supper,"(28) it seems meet and just, right and availing unto salvation, to pause for a short time in sweet contemplation of this mystery so that, enlightened by that light which shines from the Gospel and makes clearer the mystery itself, we also may be able to obtain the realization of the desire of which the Apostle of the Gentiles speaks in writing to the Ephesians. "That Christ may dwell by faith in your hearts, that being rooted and founded in charity you may be able to comprehend with all the saints what is the breadth, and length, and height, and depth; to know also the charity of Christ which surpasseth all knowledge, that you may be filled unto all the fulness of God."(29)

35. The mystery of the divine redemption is primarily and by its very nature a mystery of love, that is, of the perfect love of Christ for His heavenly Father to Whom the sacrifice of the Cross, offered in a spirit of love and obedience, presents the most abundant and infinite satisfaction due for the sins of the human race; "By suffering out of love and obedience, Christ gave more to God than was required to compensate for the offense of the whole human race."(30)

36. It is also a mystery of the love of the Most Holy Trinity and of the divine Redeemer towards all men. Because they were entirely unable

to make adequate satisfaction for their sins,(31) Christ, through the infinite treasure of His merits acquired for us by the shedding of His precious Blood, was able to restore completely that pact of friendship between God and man which had been broken, first by the grievous fall of Adam in the earthly paradise and then by the countless sins of the chosen people.

37. Since our divine Redeemer as our lawful and perfect Mediator, out of His ardent love for us, restored complete harmony between the duties and obligations of the human race and the rights of God, He is therefore responsible for the existence of that wonderful reconciliation of divine justice and divine mercy which constitutes the sublime mystery of our salvation. On this point the Angelic Doctor wisely comments: "That man should be delivered by Christ's Passion was in keeping with both His mercy and His justice. With His justice, because by His Passion Christ made satisfaction for the sins of the human race, and so man was set free by Christ's justice; and with His mercy, for since man of himself could not satisfy for the sin of all human nature, God gave him His Son to satisfy for him. And this came of a more copious mercy than if he had forgiven sins without satisfaction: Hence St. Paul says: 'God, who is rich in mercy, by reason of His very great love wherewith He has loved us even when we were dead by reason of our sins, brought us to life together with Christ.'"(32)

38. But in order that we really may be able, so far as it is permitted to mortal men, "to comprehend with all the saints what is the breadth, and length, and height, and depth"(33) of the hidden love of the Incarnate Word for His heavenly Father and for men infected by the taint of sins, we must note well that His love was not entirely the spiritual love proper to God inasmuch as "God is a spirit."(34) Undoubtedly the love with which God loved our forefathers and the Hebrew people was of this nature. For this reason the expressions of human, intimate, and paternal love which we find in the Psalms, the writings of the prophets, and in the Canticle of Canticles are tokens and symbols of the true but entirely spiritual love with which God

continued to sustain the human race. On the other hand, the love which breathes from the Gospel, from the letters of the Apostles and the pages of the Apocalypse, all of which portray the love of the Heart of Jesus Christ, expresses not only divine love but also human sentiments of love. All who profess themselves Catholics accept this without question.

39. For the Word of God did not assume a feigned and unsubstantial body, as already in the first century of Christianity some heretics declared and who were condemned in these solemn words of St. John the Apostle: "For many seducers are gone out into the world, who do confess not that Jesus Christ is come in the flesh. Here is a seducer and the antichrist,"(35) but He united to His divine Person a truly human nature, individual, whole and perfect, which was conceived in the most pure womb of the Virgin Mary by the power of the Holy Ghost.(36)

40. Nothing, then, was wanting to the human nature which the Word of God united to Himself. Consequently He assumed it in no diminished way, in no different sense in what concerns the spiritual and the corporeal: that is, it was endowed with intellect and will and the other internal and external faculties of perception, and likewise with the desires and all the natural impulses of the senses. All this the Catholic Church teaches as solemnly defined and ratified by the Roman Pontiffs and the general councils. "Whole and entire in what is His own, whole and entire in what is ours."(37) "Perfect in His Godhead and likewise perfect in His humanity."(38) "Complete God is man, complete man is God."(39)

41. Hence, since there can be no doubt that Jesus Christ received a true body and had all the affections proper to the same, among which love surpassed all the rest, it is likewise beyond doubt that He was endowed with a physical heart like ours; for without this noblest part of the body the ordinary emotions of human life are impossible. Therefore the Heart of Jesus Christ, hypostatically united to the divine Person of the Word, certainly beat with love and with the other emotions- but these,

joined to a human will full of divine charity and to the infinite love itself which the Son shares with the Father and the Holy Spirit, were in such complete unity and agreement that never among these three loves was there any contradiction of or disharmony.(40)

42. However, even though the Word of God took to Himself a true and perfect human nature, and made and fashioned for Himself a heart of flesh, which, no less than ours could suffer and be pierced, unless this fact is considered in the light of the hypostatic and substantial union and in the light of its complement, the fact of man's redemption, it can be a stumbling block and foolishness to some, just as Jesus Christ, nailed to the Cross, actually was to the Jewish race and to the Gentiles.(41)

43. The official teachings of the Catholic faith, in complete agreement with Scripture, assure us that the only begotten Son of God took a human nature capable of suffering and death especially because He desired, as He hung from the Cross, to offer a bloody sacrifice in order to complete the work of man's salvation. This the Apostle of the Gentiles teaches in another way: "For both He that sanctifieth, and they who are sanctified are all of one. For which cause He is not ashamed to call them brethren, saying, 'I will declare thy name to My brethren'. . .And again, 'Behold I and My children, whom God hath given Me.' Therefore, because the children are partakers of flesh and blood, He also in like manner hath been partaker of the same. . .Wherefore it behooved Him in all things to be made like unto His brethren that He might become a merciful and faithful high priest before God, that He might be a propitiation for the sins of the people. For in that wherein He Himself hath suffered and been tempted He is able to succor them who are tempted."(42)

44. The holy Fathers, true witnesses of the divinely revealed doctrine, wonderfully understood what St. Paul the Apostle had quite clearly declared; namely, that the mystery of love was, as it were, both the foundation and the culmination of the Incarnation and the

Redemption. For frequently and clearly we can read in their writings that Jesus Christ took a perfect human nature and our weak and perishable human body with the object of providing for our eternal salvation, and of revealing to us in the clearest possible manner that His infinite love for us could express itself in human terms.

45. St. Justin, almost echoing the voice of the Apostle of the Gentiles, writes: "We adore and love the Word born of the unbegotten and ineffable God since He became man for our sake, so that having become a partaker of our sufferings He might provide a remedy for them."(43)

46. St. Basil, the first of the three Cappadocian Fathers declares that the feelings of the senses in Christ were at once true and holy: "It is clear that the Lord did indeed put on natural affections as a proof of His real and not imaginary Incarnation, and that He rejected as unworthy of the Godhead those corrupt affections which defile the purity of our life."(44)

47. Similarly that light of the Church of Antioch, St. John Chrysostom, admits that the emotion of the senses to which the divine Redeemer was subject made obvious the fact that He assumed a human nature complete in all respects: "For if He had not shared our nature He would not have repeatedly been seized with grief."(45)

48. Among the Latin Fathers one may cite those whom the Church today honors as the greatest doctors. Thus St. Ambrose bears witness that the movements and dispositions of the senses, from which the Incarnate Word of (God was not exempt, flow from the hypostatic union as from their natural source: "And therefore He put on a soul and the passions of the soul; for God, precisely because He is God, could not have been disturbed nor could He have died."(46)

49. It was from these very emotions that St. Jerome derived his chief proof that Christ had really put on human nature: "Our Lord, to prove

the truth of the manhood He had assumed, experiences real sadness."(47)

50. But St. Augustine, in a special manner, notices the connections that exist between the sentiments of the Incarnate Word and their purpose, man's redemption. "These affections of human infirmity, even as the human body itself and death, the Lord Jesus put on not out of necessity, but freely out of compassion so that He might transform in Himself His Body, which is the Church of which He deigned to be the Head, that is, His members who are among the faithful and the saints, so that if any of them in the trials of this life should be saddened and afflicted they should not therefore think that they are deprived of His grace. Nor should they consider this sorrow a sin, but a sign of human weakness. Like a choir singing in harmony with the note that has been sounded, so should His Body learn from its Head."(48)

51. More briefly, but no less effectively, do the following passages from St. John Damascene set out the teaching of the Church: "Complete God assumed me completely and complete man is united to complete God so that He might bring salvation to complete man. For what was not assumed could not be healed."(49) "He therefore assumed all that He might sanctify all."(50)

52. However, it must be noted that although these selected passages from Scripture and the Fathers and many similar ones that We have not cited give clear testimony that Jesus Christ was endowed with affections and sense perceptions, and hence that He assumed human nature in order to work for our eternal salvation, yet they never refer those affections to His physical heart in such a way as to point to it clearly as the symbol of His infinite love.

53. Granted that the Evangelists and other sacred writers do not explicitly describe the Heart of our Redeemer, living and throbbing like our own with the power of feeling, and ever throbbing with the emotions and affections of His soul and the glowing charity of His

twofold will, yet they often set in their proper light His divine love and the sense emotions which accompany it; that is, desire, joy, weakness, fear and anger, as shown by His face, words or gesture. The face of our adorable Savior was especially the guide, and a kind of faithful reflection, of those emotions which moved His soul in various ways and like repeating waves touched His Sacred Heart and excited its beating. For what is true of human psychology and its effects is valid here also. The Angelic Doctor, relying on ordinary experience, notes: "An emotion caused by anger is conveyed to the external members, and particularly to those members in which the heart's imprint is more obviously reflected, such as the eyes, the face, and the tongue."(51)

54. For these reasons, the Heart of the Incarnate Word is deservedly and rightly considered the chief sign and symbol of that threefold love with which the divine Redeemer unceasingly loves His eternal Father and all mankind.

55. It is a symbol of that divine love which He shares with the Father and the Holy Spirit but which He, the Word made flesh, alone manifests through a weak and perishable body, since "in Him dwells the fullness of the Godhead bodily."(52)

56. It is, besides, the symbol of that burning love which, infused into His soul, enriches the human will of Christ and enlightens and governs its acts by the most perfect knowledge derived both from the beatific vision and that which is directly infused.(53)

57. And finally - and this in a more natural and direct way - it is the symbol also of sensible love, since the body of Jesus Christ, formed by the Holy Spirit, in the womb of the Virgin Mary, possesses full powers of feelings and perception, in fact, more so than any other human body.(54)

58. Since, therefore, Sacred Scripture and the official teaching of the Catholic faith instruct us that all things find their complete harmony and order in the most holy soul of Jesus Christ, and that He has

manifestly directed His threefold love for the securing of our redemption, it unquestionably follows that we can contemplate and honor the Heart of the divine Redeemer as a symbolic image of His love and a witness of our redemption and, at the same time, as a sort of mystical ladder by which we mount to the embrace of "God our Savior."(55)

59. Hence His words, actions, commands, miracles, and especially those works which manifest more clearly His love for us - such as the divine institution of the Eucharist, His most bitter sufferings and death, the loving gift of His holy Mother to us, the founding of the Church for us, and finally, the sending of the Holy Spirit upon the Apostles and upon us - all these, We say, ought to be looked upon as proofs of His threefold love.

60. Likewise we ought to meditate most lovingly on the beating of His Sacred Heart by which He seemed, as it were, to measure the time of His sojourn on earth until that final moment when, as the Evangelists testify, "crying out with a loud voice 'It is finished.', and bowing His Head, He yielded up the ghost."(56) Then it was that His heart ceased to beat and His sensible love was interrupted until the time when, triumphing over death, He rose from the tomb.

61. But after His glorified body had been re-united to the soul of the divine Redeemer, conqueror of death, His most Sacred Heart never ceased, and never will cease, to beat with calm and imperturbable pulsations. Likewise, it will never cease to symbolize the threefold love with which He is bound to His heavenly Father and the entire human race, of which He has every claim to be the mystical Head.

62. And now, venerable brethren, in order that we may be able to gather from these holy considerations abundant and salutary fruits, We desire to reflect on and briefly contemplate the manifold affections, human and divine, of our Savior Jesus Christ which His Heart made known to us during the course of His mortal life and which It still does

and will continue to do for all eternity. From the pages of the Gospel particularly there shines forth for us the light, by the brightness and strength of which we can enter into the secret places of this divine Heart and, with the Apostle of the Gentiles, gaze at "the abundant riches of (God's) grace, in his bounty towards us in Christ Jesus."(57)

63. The adorable Heart of Jesus Christ began to beat with a love at once human and divine after the Virgin Mary generously pronounced Her "Fiat"; and the Word of God, as the Apostle remarks: "coming into the world, saith, 'Sacrifice and oblation thou wouldst not; but a body thou hast fitted to Me; holocausts for sin did not please thee. Then said I, "Behold I come"; in the head of the book it is written of Me, "that I should do thy will, O God!"'. . .In which will we are sanctified by the oblation of the body of Jesus Christ once."(58)

64. Likewise was He moved by love, completely in harmony with the affections of His human will and the divine Love, when in the house of Nazareth He conversed with His most sweet Mother and His foster father, St. Joseph, in obedience to whom He performed laborious tasks in the trade of a carpenter.

65. Again, He was influenced by that threefold love, of which We spoke, during His public life: in long apostolic journeys; in the working of innumerable miracles, by which He summoned back the dead from the grave or granted health to all manner of sick persons; in enduring labors; in bearing fatigue, hunger and thirst; in the nightly watchings during which He prayed most lovingly to His Father; and finally, in His preaching and in setting forth and explaining His parables, in those particularly which deal with mercy--the lost drachma, the lost sheep, the prodigal son. By these indeed both by act and by word, as St. Gregory the Great notes, the Heart of God Itself is revealed: "Learn

the Heart of God in the words of God, that you may long more ardently for things eternal."(59)

66. But the Heart of Jesus Christ was moved by a more urgent charity when from His lips were drawn words breathing the most ardent love. Thus, to give examples: when He was gazing at the crowds weary and hungry, He exclaimed: "I have compassion upon the crowd";(60) and when He looked down on His beloved city of Jerusalem, blinded by its sins, and so destined for final ruin, He uttered this sentence: "Jerusalem, Jerusalem, thou that slayest the prophets, and stonest them that are sent unto thee, how often would I have gathered together thy children, as the hen doth gather her chickens under her wings, and thou wouldst not!"(61) And His Heart beat with love for His Father and with a holy anger when seeing the sacrilegious buying and selling taking place in the Temple, He rebuked the violators with these words: "It is written: My house shall be called a house of prayer; but you have made it a den of thieves."(62)

67. But His Heart was moved by a particularly intense love mingled with fear as He perceived the hour of His bitter torments drawing near and, expressing a natural repugnance for the approaching pains and death, He cried out: "Father, if it be possible, let this chalice pass from Me."(63) And when He was greeted by the traitor with a kiss, in love triumphant united to deepest grief, He addressed to him those words which seem to be the final invitation of His most merciful Heart to the friend who, obdurate in his wicked treachery, was about to hand Him over to His executioners: "Friend, whereto art thou come? Dost thou betray the Son of Man with a kiss?"(64) It was out of pity and the depths of His love that He spoke to the devout women as they wept for Him on His way to the unmerited penalty of the Cross: "Daughters of Jerusalem, weep not over Me, but weep for yourselves and for your children. . .For if in the green wood they do these things, what shall be done in the dry?"(65)

68. And when the divine Redeemer was hanging on the Cross, He showed that His Heart was strongly moved by different emotions - burning love, desolation, pity, longing desire, unruffled peace. The words spoken plainly indicate these emotions: "Father, forgive them;

47

they know not what they do!"(66) "My God, My God, why hast Thou forsaken Me?"(67) "Amen, I say to thee, this day thou shalt be with Me in paradise."(68) "I thirst."(69) "Father, into Thy hands I commend My spirit."(70)

69. But who can worthily depict those beatings of the divine Heart, the signs of His infinite love, of those moments when He granted men His greatest gifts: Himself in the Sacrament of the Eucharist, His most holy Mother, and the office of the priesthood shared with us?

70. Even before He ate the Last Supper with His disciples Christ Our Lord, since He knew He was about to institute the sacrament of His body and blood by the shedding of which the new covenant was to be consecrated, felt His heart roused by strong emotions, which He revealed to the Apostles in these words: "With desire have I desired to eat this Pasch with you before I suffer."(71) And these emotions were doubtless even stronger when "taking bread, He gave thanks, and broke, and gave to them, saying, 'This is My body which is given for you, this do in commemoration of Me.' Likewise the chalice also, after He had supped, saying, 'This chalice is the new testament in My blood, which shall be shed for you.'"(72)

71. It can therefore be declared that the divine Eucharist, both the sacrament which He gives to men and the sacrifice in which He unceasingly offers Himself from the rising of the sun till the going down thereof,"(73) and likewise the priesthood, are indeed gifts of the Sacred Heart of Jesus.

72. Another most precious gift of His Sacred Heart is, as We have said, Mary the beloved Mother of God and the most loving Mother of us all. She who gave birth to our Savior according to the flesh and was associated with Him in recalling the children of Eve to the life of divine grace has deservedly been hailed as the spiritual Mother of the whole human race. And so St. Augustine writes of her: "Clearly She is Mother of the members of the Savior (which is what we are), because She

labored with Him in love that the faithful who are members of the Head might be born in the Church."(74)

73. To the unbloody gift of Himself under the appearance of bread and wine our Savior Jesus Christ wished to join, as the chief proof of His deep and infinite love, the bloody sacrifice of the Cross. By this manner of acting He gave an example of His supreme charity, which He had proposed to His disciples as the highest point of love in these words: "Greater love than this no man hath, that a man lay down his life for his friends."(75)

74. Thus the love of Jesus Christ the Son of God, by the sacrifice of Golgotha, cast a flood of light on the meaning of the love of God Himself: "In this we know the charity of God, because He hath laid down His life for us, and we ought to lay down our lives for the brethren."(76) And in truth it was more by love than by the violence of the executioners that our divine Redeemer was fixed to the Cross; and His voluntary total offering is the supreme gift which He gave to each man, according to that terse saying of the Apostles, "He loved me, and delivered Himself for me."(77)

75. The Sacred Heart of Jesus shares in a most intimate way in the life of the Incarnate Word, and has been thus assumed as a kind of instrument of the Divinity. It is therefore beyond all doubt that, in the carrying out of works of grace and divine omnipotence, His Heart, no less than the other members of His human nature is also a legitimate symbol of that unbounded love.(78)

76. Under the influence of this love, our Savior, by the outpouring of His blood, became wedded to His Church: "By love, He allowed Himself to be espoused to His Church."(79) Hence, from the wounded Heart of the Redeemer was born the Church, the dispenser of the Blood of the Redemption--whence flows that plentiful stream of Sacramental grace from which the children of the Church drink of eternal life, as we read in the sacred liturgy: "From the pierced Heart,

the Church, the Bride of Christ, is born....And He pours forth grace from His Heart."(80)

77. Concerning the meaning of this symbol, which was known even to the earliest Fathers and ecclesiastical writers, St. Thomas Aquinas, echoing something of their words, writes as follows: "From the side of Christ, there flowed water for cleansing, blood for redeeming. Hence blood is associated with the sacrament of the Eucharist, water with the sacrament of Baptism, which has its cleansing power by virtue of the blood of Christ."(81)

78. What is here written of the side of Christ, opened by the wound from the soldier, should also be said of the Heart which was certainly reached by the stab of the lance, since the soldier pierced it precisely to make certain that Jesus Christ crucified was really dead. Hence the wound of the most Sacred Heart of Jesus, now that He has completed His mortal life, remains through the course of the ages a striking image of that spontaneous charity by which God gave His only begotten Son for the redemption of men and by which Christ expressed such passionate love for us that He offered Himself as a bleeding victim on Calvary for our sake: "Christ loved us and delivered Himself for us, an oblation and a sacrifice to God for an odor of sweetness."(82)

79. After our Lord had ascended into heaven with His body adorned with the splendors of eternal glory and took His place by the right hand of the Father, He did not cease to remain with His Spouse, the Church, by means of the burning love with which His Heart beats. For He bears in His hands, feet and side the glorious marks of the wounds which manifest the threefold victory won over the devil, sin, and death.

80. He likewise keeps in His Heart, locked as it were in a most precious shrine, the unlimited treasures of His merits, the fruits of that same threefold triumph, which He generously bestows on the redeemed human race. This is a truth full of consolation, which the Apostle of the Gentiles expresses in these words: "Ascending on high, He led

captivity captive; He gave gifts to men. . .He that descended, is the same also that ascended above all the heavens that He might fill all things."(83)

81. The gift of the Holy Spirit, sent upon His disciples, is the first notable sign of His abounding charity after His triumphant ascent to the right hand of His Father. For after ten days the Holy Spirit, given by the heavenly Father, came down upon them gathered in the Upper Room in accordance with the promise made at the Last Supper: "I will ask the Father and He will give you another Paraclete so that He may abide with you forever."(84) And this Paraclete, who is the mutual personal love between the Father and the Son, is sent by both and, under the adopted appearance of tongues of fire, poured into their souls an abundance of divine charity and the other heavenly gifts.

82. The infusion of this divine charity also has its origin in the Heart of the Savior, "in which are hid all the treasures of wisdom and knowledge."(85) For this charity is the gift of Jesus Christ and of His Spirit; for He is indeed the spirit of the Father and the Son from whom the origin of the Church and its marvelous extension is revealed to all the pagan races which had been defiled by idolatry, family hatred, corrupt morals, and violence.

83. This divine charity is the most precious gift of the Heart of Christ and of His Spirit: It is this which imparted to the Apostles and martyrs that fortitude, by the strength of which they fought their battles like heroes till death in order to preach the truth of the Gospel and bear witness to it by the shedding of their blood; it is this which implanted in the Doctors of the Church their intense zeal for explaining and defending the Catholic faith; this nourished the virtues of the confessors, and roused them to those marvelous works useful for their own salvation and beneficial to the salvation of others both in this life and in the next; this, finally, moved the virgins to a free and joyful withdrawal from the pleasures of the senses and to the complete dedication of themselves to the love of their heavenly Spouse.

84. It was to pay honor to this divine charity which, overflowing from the Heart of the Incarnate Word, is poured out by the aid of the Holy Spirit into the souls of all believers that the Apostle of the Gentiles uttered this hymn of triumph which proclaims the victory of Christ the Head, and of the members of His Mystical Body, over all which might in any way impede the establishment of the kingdom of love among men: "Who shall separate us from the love of Christ? Shall tribulation or distress? or famine? or nakedness? or danger? or persecution? or the sword?. . .But in all these things we overcome because of Him that hath loved us. For I am sure that neither death nor life, nor angels nor principalities, nor powers, nor things present, nor things to come, nor might, nor height nor depth, nor any other creature shall be able to separate us from the love of God, which is in Christ Jesus our Lord."(86)

85. Nothing therefore prevents our adoring the Sacred Heart of Jesus Christ as having a part in and being the natural and expressive symbol of the abiding love with which the divine Redeemer is still on fire for mankind. Though it is no longer subject to the varying emotions of this mortal life, yet it lives and beats and is united inseparably with the Person of the divine Word and, in Him and through Him, with the divine Will. Since then the Heart of Christ is overflowing with love both human and divine and rich with the treasure of all graces which our Redeemer acquired by His life, sufferings and death, it is therefore the enduring source of that charity which His Spirit pours forth on all the members of His Mystical Body.

86. And so the Heart of our Savior reflects in some way the image of the divine Person of the Word and, at the same time, of His twofold nature, the human and the divine; in it we can consider not only the symbol but, in a sense, the summary of the whole mystery of our redemption. When we adore the Sacred Heart of Jesus Christ, we adore in it and through it both the uncreated love of the divine Word and also its human love and its other emotions and virtues, since both loves moved our Redeemer to sacrifice Himself for us and for His Spouse,

the Universal Church, as the Apostle declares: "Christ loved the Church, and delivered Himself up for it, that He might sanctify it, cleansing it by the laver of water in the word of life, that He might present it to Himself a glorious Church, not having spot or wrinkle, or any such thing, but that it should be holy and without blemish."(87)

87. Just as Christ loved the Church, so He still loves it most intensely with that threefold love of which We spoke, which moved Him as our Advocate (88) "always living to make intercession for us"(89) to win grace and mercy for us from His Father. The prayers which are drawn from that unfailing love, and are directed to the Father, never cease. As "in the days of His flesh,"(90) so now victorious in heaven, He makes His petition to His heavenly Father with equal efficacy, to Him "Who so loved the world that He gave His only begotten Son, that whosoever believeth in Him may not perish, but may have life everlasting,"(91) He shows His living Heart, wounded as it were, and throbbing with a love yet more intense than when it was wounded in death by the Roman soldier's lance: "(Thy Heart) has been wounded so that through the visible wound we may behold the invisible wound of love."(92)

88. It is beyond doubt, then, that His heavenly Father "Who spared not even His own Son, but delivered Him up for us all,"(93) when appealed to with such loving urgency by so powerful an Advocate, will, through Him, send down on all men an abundance of divine graces.

89. It was Our wish, venerable brethren, by this general outline, to set before you and the faithful the inner nature of the devotion to the Sacred Heart of Jesus Christ and the endless riches which spring from it as they are made clear by the primary source of doctrine, divine revelation. We think that Our comments, which are guided by the light of the Gospel, have proved that this devotion, summarily expressed, is nothing else than devotion to the divine and human love of the Incarnate Word and to the love by which the heavenly Father and the Holy Spirit exercise their care over sinful men. For, as the Angelic

Doctor teaches, the love of the most Holy Trinity is the origin of man's redemption; it overflowed into the human will of Jesus Christ and into His adorable Heart with full efficacy and led Him, under the impulse of that love, to pour forth His blood to redeem us from the captivity of sin(94): "I have a baptism wherewith I am to be baptized, and how am I straitened until it be accomplished?"(95)

90. We are convinced, then, that the devotion which We are fostering to the love of God and Jesus Christ for the human race by means of the revered symbol of the pierced Heart of the crucified Redeemer has never been altogether unknown to the piety of the faithful, although it has become more clearly known and has spread in a remarkable manner throughout the Church in quite recent times. Particularly was this so after our Lord Himself had privately revealed this divine secret to some of His children to whom He had granted an abundance of heavenly gifts, and whom He had chosen as His special messengers and heralds of this devotion.

91. But, in fact, there have always been men specially dedicated to God who, following the example of the beloved Mother of God, of the Apostles and the great Fathers of the Church, have practiced the devotion of thanksgiving, adoration and love towards the most sacred human nature of Christ, and especially towards the wounds by which His body was torn when He was enduring suffering for our salvation.

92. Moreover, is there not contained in those words "My Lord and My God"(96) which St. Thomas the Apostle uttered, and which showed he had been changed from an unbeliever into a faithful follower, a profession of faith, adoration and love, mounting up from the wounded human nature of his Lord to the majesty of the divine Person?

93. But if men have always been deeply moved by the pierced Heart of the Savior to a worship of that infinite love with which He embraces mankind -- since the words of the prophet Zacharias, "They shall look

on Him Whom they have pierced,"(97) referred by St. John the Evangelist to Jesus nailed to the Cross, have been spoken to Christians in all ages -- it must yet be admitted that it was only by a very gradual advance that the honors of a special devotion were offered to that Heart as depicting the love, human and divine, which exists in the Incarnate Word.

94. But for those who wish to touch on the more significant stages of this devotion through the centuries, if we consider outward practice, there immediately occur the names of certain individuals who have won particular renown in this matter as being the advance guard of a form of piety which, privately and very gradually, has gained more and more strength in religious congregations. To cite some examples in establishing this devotion to the Sacred Heart of Jesus and continuously promoting it, great service was rendered by St. Bonaventure, St. Albert the Great, St. Gertrude, St. Catherine of Siena, Blessed Henry Suso, St. Peter Canisius, St. Francis de Sales. St. John Eudes was responsible for the first liturgical office celebrated in honor of the Sacred Heart of Jesus whose solemn feast, with the approval of many Bishops in France, was observed for the first time on October 20th, 1672.

95. But surely the most distinguished place among those who have fostered this most excellent type of devotion is held by St. Margaret Mary Alacoque who, under the spiritual direction of Blessed Claude de la Colombiere who assisted her work, was on fire with an unusual zeal to see to it that the real meaning of the devotion which had had such extensive developments to the great edification of the faithful should be established and be distinguished from other forms of Christian piety by the special qualities of love and reparation.(98)

96. It is enough to recall the record of that age in which the devotion to the Sacred Heart of Jesus began to develop to understand clearly that its marvelous progress has stemmed from the fact that it entirely agreed with the nature of Christian piety since it was a devotion of

love. It must not be said that this devotion has taken its origin from some private revelation of God and has suddenly appeared in the Church; rather, it has blossomed forth of its own accord as a result of that lively faith and burning devotion of men who were endowed with heavenly gifts, and who were drawn towards the adorable Redeemer and His glorious wounds which they saw as irresistible proofs of that unbounded love.

97. Consequently, it is clear that the revelations made to St. Margaret Mary brought nothing new into Catholic doctrine. Their importance lay in this that Christ Our Lord, exposing His Sacred Heart, wished in a quite extraordinary way to invite the minds of men to a contemplation of, and a devotion to, the mystery of God's merciful love for the human race. In this special manifestation Christ pointed to His Heart, with definite and repeated words, as the symbol by which men should be attracted to a knowledge and recognition of His love; and at the same time He established it as a sign or pledge of mercy and grace for the needs of the Church of our times.

98. In addition, that this devotion flows from the very foundations of Christian teaching is clearly shown by the fact that the Apostolic See approved the liturgical feast before it approved the writings of St. Margaret Mary; for without exactly taking account of any private revelation from God, but rather graciously acceding to the petitions of the faithful, the Sacred Congregation of Rites - by a decree of the 25th of January 1765, which was approved by Our predecessor, Clement XIII, on the 6th of February of the same year - granted the liturgical celebration of the feast to the Polish Bishops and to what was called the Archconfraternity of the Sacred Heart of Jesus at Rome. The Apostolic See acted in this way so that the devotion then existing and flourishing might be extended, since its purpose was "by this symbol to renew the memory of that divine love"(99) by which Our Savior was moved to offer Himself as a victim atoning for the sins of men.

99. This first approval, granted as a privilege and restricted within limits, was followed about a century later by another of far greater importance and couched in more solemn terms. We mean the decree, which We referred to above, of the Sacred Congregation of Rites of the 23rd of August 1856 by which Our predecessor of immortal memory, Pius IX, in answer to the prayer of the French Bishops and of almost the whole Catholic world, extended the feast of the Sacred Heart of Jesus to the Universal Church and ordered it to be fittingly observed.(100) This act richly deserved to be commended to the lasting memory of the faithful, for as we read in the liturgy of the same feast: "From that time the devotion to the Sacred Heart, like a stream in flood sweeping aside all obstacles, spread out over the whole world."

100. From what We have so far explained, venerable brethren, it is clear that the faithful must seek from Scripture, tradition and the sacred liturgy as from a deep untainted source, the devotion to the Sacred Heart of Jesus if they desire to penetrate its inner nature and by piously meditating on it, receive the nourishment for the fostering and development of their religious fervor. If this devotion is constantly practiced with this knowledge and understanding, the souls of the faithful cannot but attain to the sweet knowledge of the love of Christ which is the perfection of Christian life as the Apostle, who knew this from personal experience, teaches: "For this cause I bow my knees to the Father of our Lord Jesus Christ. . . that He may grant you, according to the riches of His glory, to be strengthened by His Spirit with might unto the inward man; that Christ may dwell by faith in your hearts; that, being rooted and founded in charity. . .you may be able to know also the charity of Christ which surpasseth all knowledge, that you may be filled unto all the fullness of God."(101) The clearest image of this all-embracing fullness of God is the Heart of Christ Jesus Itself. We mean the fullness of mercy which is proper to the New Testament, in which "the goodness and kindness of God our Savior appeared,"(102) for "God sent not His Son into the world to judge the world, but that the world might be saved by Him."(103)

101. The Church, the teacher of men, has therefore always been convinced from the time she first published official documents concerning the devotion to the Sacred Heart of Jesus that its essential elements, namely, acts of love and reparation by which God's infinite love for the human race is honored, are in no sense tinged with so-called "materialism" or tainted with the poison of superstition. Rather, this devotion is a form of piety that fully corresponds to the true spiritual worship which the Savior Himself foretold when speaking to the woman of Samaria: "The hour cometh, and now is, when the true adorers shall adore the Father in spirit and in truth. For the Father also seeketh such to adore Him. God is a spirit; and they that adore Him must adore Him in spirit and in truth."(104)

102. It is wrong, therefore, to assert that the contemplation of the physical Heart of Jesus prevents an approach to a close love of God and holds back the soul on the way to the attainment of the highest virtues. This false mystical doctrine the Church emphatically rejects as, speaking through Our predecessor of happy memory, Innocent XI, she rejected the errors of those who foolishly declared: "(Souls of this interior way) ought not to make acts of love for the Blessed Virgin, the Saints or the humanity of Christ; for love directed towards those is of the senses, since its objects are also of that kind. No creature, neither the Blessed Virgin nor the Saints, ought to have a place in our heart, because God alone wishes to occupy it and possess it."(105) It is obvious that those who think in this way imagine that the image of the Heart of Jesus represents His human love alone and that there is nothing in it on which, as on a new foundation, the worship of adoration which is exclusively reserved to the divine nature can be based. But everyone realizes that this interpretation of sacred images is entirely false, since it obviously restricts their meaning much too narrowly.

103. Quite the contrary is the thought and teaching of Catholic theologians, among whom St. Thomas writes as follows: "Religious worship is not paid to images, considered in themselves, as things; but

according as they are representations leading to God Incarnate. The approach which is made to the image as such does not stop there, but continues towards that which is represented. Hence, because a religious honor is paid to the images of Christ, it does not therefore mean that there are different degrees of supreme worship or of the virtue of religion."(106) It is, then, to the Person of the divine Word as to its final object that that devotion is directed which, in a relative sense, is observed towards the images whether those images are relics of the bitter sufferings which our Savior endured for our sake or that particular image which surpasses all the rest in efficacy and meaning, namely, the pierced Heart of the crucified Christ.

104. Thus, from something corporeal such as the Heart of Jesus Christ with its natural meaning, it is both lawful and fitting for us, supported by Christian faith, to mount not only to its love as perceived by the senses but also higher, to a consideration and adoration of the infused heavenly love; and finally, by a movement of the soul at once sweet and sublime, to reflection on, and adoration of, the divine love of the Word Incarnate. We do so since, in accordance with the faith by which we believe that both natures - the human and the divine - are united in the Person of Christ, we can grasp in our minds those most intimate ties which unite the love of feeling of the physical Heart of Jesus with that twofold spiritual love, namely, the human and the divine love. For these loves must be spoken of not only as existing side by side in the adorable Person of the divine Redeemer but also as being linked together by a natural bond insofar as the human love, including that of the feelings, is subject to the divine and, in due proportion, provides us with an image of the latter. We do not pretend, however, that we must contemplate and adore in the Heart of Jesus what is called the formal image, that is to say, the perfect and absolute symbol of His divine love, for no created image is capable of adequately expressing the essence of this love. But a Christian in paying honor along with the Church to the Heart of Jesus is adoring the symbol and, as it were, the visible sign of the divine charity which went so far as to love intensely,

through the Heart of the Word made Flesh, the human race stained with so many sins.

105. It is therefore essential, at this point, in a doctrine of such importance and requiring such prudence that each one constantly hold that the truth of the natural symbol by which the physical Heart of Jesus is related to the Person of the Word, entirely depends upon the fundamental truth of the hypostatic union. Should anyone declare this to be untrue he would be reviving false opinions, more than once condemned by the Church, for they are opposed to the oneness of the Person of Christ even though the two natures are each complete and distinct.

106. Once this essential truth has been established we understand that the Heart of Jesus is the heart of a divine Person, the Word Incarnate, and by it is represented and, as it were, placed before our gaze all the love with which He has embraced and even now embraces us. Consequently, the honor to be paid to the Sacred Heart is such as to raise it to the rank - so far as external practice is concerned - of the highest expression of Christian piety. For this is the religion of Jesus which is centered on the Mediator who is man and God, and in such a way that we cannot reach the Heart of God save through the Heart of Christ, as He Himself says: "I am the Way, the Truth and the Life. No one cometh to the Father save by Me."(107)

107. And so we can easily understand that the devotion to the Sacred Heart of Jesus, of its very nature, is a worship of the love with which God, through Jesus, loved us, and at the same time, an exercise of our own love by which we are related to God and to other men. Or to express it in another way, devotion of this kind is directed towards the love of God for us in order to adore it, give thanks for it, and live so as to imitate it; it has this in view, as the end to be attained, that we bring that love by which we are bound to God to the rest of men to perfect fulfillment by carrying out daily more eagerly the new commandment which the divine Master gave to His Apostles as a

sacred legacy when He said: "A new commandment I give to you, that you love one another as I have loved you. . .This is My commandment that you love one another as I have loved you."(108) And this commandment is really new and Christ's own, for as Aquinas says, "It is, in brief, the difference between the New and the Old Testament, for as Jeremias says, 'I will make a new covenant with the house of Israel.'(109) But that commandment which in the Old Testament was based on fear and reverential love was referring to the New Testament; hence, this commandment was in the old Law not really belonging to it, but as a preparation for the new Law."(110)

108. Before We conclude Our treatment of the concept of this type of devotion and its excellence in Christian life, which We have offered for your consideration - a subject at once attractive and full of consolation - by virtue of the Apostolic office which was first entrusted to Blessed Peter after he had made his threefold profession of love, We think it opportune to exhort you once again venerable brethren, and through you all those dear children of Ours in Christ, to continue to exercise an ever more vigorous zeal in promoting this most attractive form of piety; for from it in our times also We trust that very many benefits will arise.

109. In truth, if the arguments brought forward which form the foundation for the devotion to the pierced Heart of Jesus are duly pondered, it is surely clear that there is no question here of some ordinary form of piety which anyone at his own whim may treat as of little consequence or set aside as inferior to others, but of a religious practice which helps very much towards the attaining of Christian perfection. For if "devotion" - according to the accepted theological notion which the Angelic Doctor gives us - "appears to be nothing else save a willingness to give oneself readily to what concerns the service of God,"(111) is it possible that there is any service of God more obligatory and necessary, and at the same time more excellent and attractive, than the one which is dedicated to love? For what is more pleasing and acceptable to God than service which pays homage to the

divine love and is offered for the sake of that love--since any service freely offered is a gift in some sense and love "has the position of the first gift, through which all other free gifts are made?"(112)

110. That form of piety, then, should be held in highest esteem by means of which man honors and loves God more and dedicates himself with greater ease and promptness to the divine charity; a form which our Redeemer Himself deigned to propose and commend to Christians and which the Supreme Pontiffs in their turn defended and highly praised in memorable published documents. Consequently, to consider of little worth this signal benefit conferred on the Church by Jesus Christ would be to do something both rash and harmful and also deserving of God's displeasure.

111. This being so, there is no doubt that Christians in paying homage to the Sacred Heart of the Redeemer are fulfilling a serious part of their obligations in their service of God and, at the same time, they are surrendering themselves to their Creator and Redeemer with regard to both the affections of the heart and the external activities of their life; in this way, they are obeying that divine commandment: "Thou shalt love the Lord thy God with thy whole heart, and with thy whole soul, and with thy whole mind, and with thy whole Strength."(113)

112. Besides, they have the firm conviction that they are moved to honor God not primarily for their own advantage in what concerns soul and body in this life and in the next, but for the sake of God's goodness they strive to render Him their homage, to give Him back love for love, to adore Him and offer Him due thanks. Were it not so, the devotion to the Sacred Heart of Jesus Christ would be out of harmony with the whole spirit of the Christian religion, since man would not direct his homage, in the first instance, to the divine love. And, not unreasonably as sometimes happens, accusations of excessive self-love and self-interest are made against those who either misunderstand this excellent form of piety or practice it in the wrong way. Hence, let all be completely convinced that in showing devotion

to the most Sacred Heart of Jesus the external acts of piety have not the first or most important place; nor is its essence to be found primarily in the benefits to be obtained. For if Christ has solemnly promised them in private revelations it was for the purpose of encouraging men to perform with greater fervor the chief duties of the Catholic religion, namely, love and expiation, and thus take all possible measures for their own spiritual advantage.

113. We therefore urge all Our children in Christ, both those who are already accustomed to drink the saving waters flowing from the Heart of the Redeemer and, more especially those who look on from a distance like hesitant spectators, to eagerly embrace this devotion. Let them carefully consider, as We have said, that it is a question of a devotion which has long been powerful in the Church and is solidly founded on the Gospel narrative. It received clear support from tradition and the sacred liturgy and has been frequently and generously praised by the Roman Pontiffs themselves. These were not satisfied with establishing a feast in honor of the most Sacred Heart of the Redeemer and extending it to the Universal Church; they were also responsible for the solemn acts of dedication which consecrated the whole human race to the same Sacred Heart.(114)

114. Moreover, there are to be reckoned the abundant and joyous fruits which have flowed therefrom to the Church: countless souls returned to the Christian religion, the faith of many roused to greater activity, a closer tie between the faithful and our most loving Redeemer. All these benefits particularly in the most recent decades, have passed before Our eyes in greater numbers and more dazzling significance.

115. While We gaze round at such a marvelous sight, namely, a devotion to the Sacred Heart of Jesus both warm and widespread among all ranks of the faithful, We are filled with a sense of gratitude and joy and consolation. And after We have offered thanks, as We ought, to our Redeemer Who is the infinite treasury of goodness, We cannot help offering Our paternal congratulations to all those, whether

of the clergy or of the laity, who have made active contribution to the extending of this devotion.

116. But although, venerable brethren, devotion to the Sacred Heart of Jesus has everywhere brought forth fruits of salvation for the Christian life, all are aware that the Church militant on earth -and especially civil society - has not yet attained in a real sense to its essential perfection which would correspond to the prayers and desires of Jesus Christ, the Mystical Spouse of the Church and Redeemer of the human race. Not a few children of the Church mar, by their too many sins and imperfections, the beauty of this Mother's features which they reflect in themselves. Not all Christians are distinguished by that holiness of behavior to which God calls them; not all sinners have returned to the Father ' s house, which they unfortunately abandoned, that they may be clothed once again with the "first robe"(115) and worthily receive on their finger the ring, the pledge of loyalty to the spouse of their soul; not all the heathen peoples have yet been gathered into the membership of the Mystical Body of Christ.

117. And there is more. For if We experience bitter sorrow at the feeble loyalty of the good in whose souls, tricked by a deceptive desire for earthly possessions, the fire of divine charity grows cool and gradually dies out, much more is Our heart deeply grieved by the machinations of evil men who, as if instigated by Satan himself, are now more than ever zealous in their open and implacable hatred against God, against the Church and above all against him who on earth represents the Person of the divine Redeemer and exhibits His love towards men, in accordance with that well-known saying of the Doctor of Milan: "For (Peter) is being questioned about that which is uncertain, though the Lord is not uncertain; He is questioning not that He may learn, but that He may teach the one whom, at His ascent into Heaven, He was leaving to us as 'the representative of His love.'"(116)

118. But, in truth, hatred of God and of those who lawfully act in His place is the greatest kind of sin that can be committed by man created

in the image and likeness of God and destined to enjoy His perfect and enduring friendship for ever in heaven. Man, by hatred of God more than by anything else, is cut off from the Highest Good and is driven to cast aside from himself and from those near to him whatever has its origin in God, whatever is united with God, whatever leads to the enjoyment of God, that is, truth, virtue, peace and justice.(117)

119. Since then, alas, one can see that the number of those whose boast is that they are God's enemies is in some places increasing, that the false slogans of materialism are being spread by act and argument, and unbridled license for unlawful desires is everywhere being praised, is it remarkable that love, which is the supreme law of the Christian religion, the surest foundation of true and perfect justice and the chief source of peace and innocent pleasures, loses its warmth in the souls of many? For as our Savior warned us: "Because iniquity hath abounded, the charity of many shall grow cold."(118)

120. When so many evils meet Our gaze - such as cause sharp conflict among individuals, families, nations and the whole world, particularly today more than at any other time - where are We to seek a remedy, venerable brethren? Can a form of devotion surpassing that to the most Sacred Heart of Jesus be found, which corresponds better to the essential character of the Catholic faith, which is more capable of assisting the present-day needs of the Church and the human race? What religious practice is more excellent, more attractive, more salutary than this, since the devotion in question is entirely directed towards the love of God itself?(119) Finally, what more effectively than the love of Christ - which devotion to the Sacred Heart of Jesus daily increases and fosters more and more - can move the faithful to bring into the activities of life the Law of the Gospel, the setting aside of which, as the words of the Holy Spirit plainly warn, "the work of justice shall be peace,"(120) makes peace worthy of the name completely impossible among men?

121. And so, following in the footsteps of Our immediate predecessor, We are pleased to address once again to all Our dear sons in Christ those words of exhortation which Leo XIII, of immortal memory, towards the close of last century addressed to all the faithful and to all who were genuinely anxious about their own salvation and that of civil society: "Behold, today, another true sign of God's favor is presented to our gaze, namely, the Sacred Heart of Jesus. . .shining forth with a wondrous splendor from amidst flames. In it must all our hopes be placed; from it salvation is to be sought and hoped for."(121)

122. It is likewise Our most fervent desire that all who profess themselves Christians and are seriously engaged in the effort to establish the kingdom of Christ on earth will consider the practice of devotion to the Heart of Jesus as the source and symbol of unity, salvation and peace. Let no one think, however, that by such a practice anything is taken from the other forms of piety with which Christian people, under the guidance of the Church, have honored the divine Redeemer. Quite the opposite. Fervent devotional practice towards the Heart of Jesus will beyond all doubt foster and advance devotion to the Holy Cross in particular, and love for the Most Holy Sacrament of the Altar. We can even assert - as the revelations made by Jesus Christ to St. Gertrude and to St. Margaret Mary clearly show - that no one really ever has a proper understanding of Christ crucified to whom the inner mysteries of His Heart have not been made known. Nor will it be easy to understand the strength of the love which moved Christ to give Himself to us as our spiritual food save by fostering in a special way the devotion to the Eucharistic Heart of Jesus, the purpose of which is - to use the words of Our predecessor of happy memory, Leo XIII - "to call to mind the act of supreme love whereby our Redeemer, pouring forth all the treasures of His Heart in order to remain with us till the end of time, instituted the adorable Sacrament of the Eucharist."(122) For "not the least part of the revelation of that Heart is the Eucharist, which He gave to us out of the great charity of His own Heart."(123)

123. Finally, moved by an earnest desire to set strong bulwarks against the wicked designs of those who hate God and the Church and, at the same time, to lead men back again, in their private and public life, to a love of God and their neighbor, We do not hesitate to declare that devotion to the Sacred Heart of Jesus is the most effective school of the love of God; the love of God, We say, which must be the foundation on which to build the kingdom of God in the hearts of individuals, families, and nations, as that same predecessor of pious memory wisely reminds us: "The reign of Jesus Christ takes its strength and form from divine love: to love with holiness and order is its foundation and its perfection. From it these must flow: to perform duties without blame; to take away nothing of another's right; to guide the lower human affairs by heavenly principles; to give the love of God precedence over all other creatures."(124)

124. In order that favors in greater abundance may flow on all Christians, nay, on the whole human race, from the devotion to the most Sacred Heart of Jesus, let the faithful see to it that to this devotion the Immaculate Heart of the Mother of God is closely joined. For, by God's Will, in carrying out the work of human Redemption the Blessed Virgin Mary was inseparably linked with Christ in such a manner that our salvation sprang from the love and the sufferings of Jesus Christ to which the love and sorrows of His Mother were intimately united. It is, then, entirely fitting that the Christian people - who received the divine life from Christ through Mary - after they have paid their debt of honor to the Sacred Heart of Jesus should also offer to the most loving Heart of their heavenly Mother the corresponding acts of piety affection, gratitude and expiation. Entirely in keeping with this most sweet and wise disposition of divine Providence is the memorable act of consecration by which We Ourselves solemnly dedicated Holy Church and the whole world to the spotless Heart of the Blessed Virgin Mary.(125)

125. Since in the course of this year there is completed, as We mentioned above, the first hundred years since the Universal Church,

by order of Our predecessor of happy memory, Pius IX, celebrated the feast of the Sacred Heart of Jesus, We earnestly desire, venerable brethren, that the memory of this centenary be everywhere observed by the faithful in the making of public acts of adoration, thanksgiving and expiation to the divine Heart of Jesus. And though all Christian peoples will be linked by the bonds of charity and prayer in common, ceremonies of Christian joy and piety will assuredly be carried out with a special religious fervor in that nation in which, according to the dispensation of the divine Will, a holy virgin pointed the way and was the untiring herald of that devotion.

126. Meanwhile, refreshed by sweet hope and foreseeing already those spiritual fruits which We are confident will spring up in abundance in the Church from the devotion to the Sacred Heart of Jesus -provided it is correctly understood according to Our explanation and actively put into practice - We make Our prayer to God that He may graciously deign to assist these ardent desires of Ours by the strong help of His grace. May it come about, by the divine inspiration as a token of His favor, that out of the celebration established for this year the love of the faithful may grow daily more and more towards the Sacred Heart of Jesus and its sweet and sovereign kingdom be extended more widely to all in every part of the world: the kingdom "of truth and life; the kingdom of grace and holiness; the kingdom of justice, love and peace."(126)

127. As a pledge of these favors with a full heart We impart to each one of you, venerable brethren, together with the clergy and faithful committed to your charge, to those in particular who by their devoted labors foster and promote the devotion to the Sacred Heart of Jesus, Our apostolic benediction.

Given at Rome, at St. Peter's, the 15th of May, 1956, the eighteenth year of Our Pontificate.

12 PROMISES OF DEVOTION TO THE SACRED HEART OF JESUS

Our Lord Jesus Christ appeared to St. Margaret Mary between 1673-1675. Among the words spoken to her, she heard Jesus make 12 promises to those who would respond to the pleading of His Heart and make an effort to return His love. St. Margaret Mary once said, "I do not know of any other exercise in the spiritual life that is more calculated to raise a soul in a short amount of time to the height of perfection and to make it taste the true sweetness to be found in the service of Jesus Christ."

1. I will give them all the graces necessary in their state of life.
2. I will establish peace in their homes.
3. I will comfort them in all their afflictions.
4. I will be their secure refuge during life, and above all, in death.
5. I will bestow abundant blessings upon all their undertakings.
6. Sinners will find in My Heart the source and infinite ocean of mercy.
7. Lukewarm souls shall become fervent.
8. Fervent souls shall quickly mount to high perfection.
9. I will bless every place in which an image of My Heart is exposed and honored.
10. I will give to priests the gift of touching the most hardened hearts.
11. Those who shall promote this devotion shall have their names written in My Heart.
12. I promise you in the excessive mercy of My Heart that My all powerful love will grant to all those who receive Holy Communion on the First Fridays in nine consecutive months the grace of final perseverance; they shall not die in My disgrace, nor without receiving their sacraments. My divine Heart shall be their safe refuge in this last moment.

PRAYER OF REPARATION TO THE SACRED HEART OF JESUS

O sweetest Jesus, whose overflowing charity towards men is most ungratefully repaid by such great forgetfulness, neglect and contempt, see, prostrate before Thy altars, we strive by special honor to make amends for the wicked coldness of men and the contumely with which Thy most loving Heart is everywhere treated.

At the same time, mindful of the fact that we too have sometimes not been free from unworthiness, and moved therefore with most vehement sorrow, in the first place we implore Thy mercy on us, being prepared by voluntary expiation to make amends for the sins we have ourselves committed, and also for the sins of those who wander far from the way of salvation, whether because, being obstinate in their unbelief, they refuse to follow Thee as their shepherd and leader, or because, spurning the promises of their Baptism, they have cast off the most sweet yoke of Thy law. We now endeavor to expiate all these lamentable crimes together, and it is also our purpose to make amends for each one of them severally: for the want of modesty in life and dress, for impurities, for so many snares set for the minds of the innocent, for the violation of feast days, for the horrid blasphemies against Thee and Thy saints, for the insults offered to Thy Vicar and to the priestly order, for the neglect of the Sacrament of Divine love or its profanation by horrible sacrileges, and lastly for the public sins of nations which resist the rights and the teaching authority of the Church which Thou hast instituted. Would that we could wash away these crimes with our own blood! And now, to make amends for the outrage offered to the Divine honor, we offer to Thee the same satisfaction which Thou didst once offer to Thy Father on the Cross and which Thou dost continually renew on our altars, we offer this conjoined with the expiations of the Virgin Mother and of all the Saints, and of all pious Christians, promising from our heart that so far as in us lies, with the help of Thy grace, we will make amends for our own past sins, and for the sins of others, and for the neglect of Thy boundless love, by firm faith, by a pure way of life, and by a perfect observance of the Gospel law, especially that of charity; we will also strive with all our strength to prevent injuries being offered to Thee, and gather as many as we can to become Thy followers. Receive, we beseech Thee, O most benign Jesus, by the intercession of the Blessed Virgin Mary, the Reparatress, the voluntary homage of this expiation, and vouchsafe, by that great gift of final perseverance, to keep us most faithful until death in our duty and in Thy service, so that at length we may all come to that fatherland, where Thou with the Father and the Holy Ghost livest and reignest God for ever and ever. Amen.

LITANY OF THE SACRED HEART

Lord, have mercy   Lord, have mercy.
Christ, have mercy   Christ, have mercy.
Lord, have mercy   Lord, have mercy.

Christ, hear us   Christ, hear us.
Christ, graciously hear us.   Christ, graciously hear us.

God the Father of Heaven,	have mercy on us.
God the Son, Redeemer of the world,	have mercy on us.
God, the Holy Spirit,	have mercy on us.
Holy Trinity, One God,	have mercy on us.
Heart of Jesus, Son of the Eternal Father,	have mercy on us.
Heart of Jesus, formed by the Holy Spirit in the womb of the Virgin Mother,	have mercy on us.
Heart of Jesus, substantially united to the Word of God,	have mercy on us.
Heart of Jesus, of Infinite Majesty,	have mercy on us.
Heart of Jesus, Sacred Temple of God,	have mercy on us.
Heart of Jesus, Tabernacle of the Most High,	have mercy on us.
Heart of Jesus, House of God and Gate of Heaven,	have mercy on us.
Heart of Jesus, burning furnace of charity,	have mercy on us.
Heart of Jesus, abode of justice and love,	have mercy on us.
Heart of Jesus, full of goodness and love,	have mercy on us.
Heart of Jesus, abyss of all virtues,	have mercy on us.
Heart of Jesus, most worthy of all praise,	have mercy on us.
Heart of Jesus, king and center of all hearts,	have mercy on us.
Heart of Jesus, in whom are all treasures of wisdom and knowledge,	have mercy on us.
Heart of Jesus, in whom dwells the fullness of divinity,	have mercy on us.
Heart of Jesus, in whom the Father was well pleased,	have mercy on us.
Heart of Jesus, of whose fullness we have all received,	have mercy on us.

Heart of Jesus, desire of the everlasting hills, have mercy on us.
Heart of Jesus, patient and most merciful, have mercy on us.
Heart of Jesus, enriching all who invoke Thee, have mercy on us.
Heart of Jesus, fountain of life and holiness, have mercy on us.
Heart of Jesus, propitiation for our sins, have mercy on us.
Heart of Jesus, loaded down with opprobrium, have mercy on us.
Heart of Jesus, bruised for our offenses, have mercy on us.
Heart of Jesus, obedient to death, have mercy on us.
Heart of Jesus, pierced with a lance, have mercy on us.
Heart of Jesus, source of all consolation, have mercy on us.
Heart of Jesus, our life and resurrection, have mercy on us.
Heart of Jesus, our peace and our reconciliation, have mercy on us.
Heart of Jesus, victim for our sins, have mercy on us.
Heart of Jesus, salvation of those
who trust in Thee, have mercy on us.
Heart of Jesus, hope of those who die in Thee, have mercy on us.
Heart of Jesus, delight of all the Saints, have mercy on us.

V. Lamb of God, who taketh away the sins of the world,
R. spare us, O Lord.

V. Lamb of God, who taketh away the sins of the world,
R. graciously hear us, O Lord.

V. Lamb of God, who taketh away the sins of the world,
R. have mercy on us, O Lord.

V. Jesus, meek and humble of heart.
R. Make our hearts like to Thine.

Let us pray:
Almighty and eternal God, look upon the Heart of Thy most beloved Son and upon the praises and satisfaction which He offers Thee in the name of sinners; and to those who implore Thy mercy, in Thy great goodness, grant forgiveness in the name of the same Jesus Christ, Thy Son, who livest and reignest with Thee forever and ever. Amen.

PRAYER OF CONSECRATION TO THE SACRED HEART BY POPE LEO XIII

Most sweet Jesus, redeemer of the human race, look down upon us, humbly prostrate before your altar. We are yours and yours we wish to be; but to be more surely united with you, behold each one of us freely consecrates himself today to your most sacred heart. Many, indeed, have never known you, many too, despising your precepts, have rejected you. Have mercy on them all, most merciful Jesus, and draw them to your sacred heart. Be you king, O Lord, not only of the faithful who have never forsaken you, but also of the prodigal children who have abandoned you; grant that they may quickly return to their father's house, lest they die of wretchedness and hunger. Be you king of those who are deceived by erroneous opinions, or whom discord keeps aloof, and call them back to the harbor of truth and unity of faith, so that soon there may be but one flock and one shepherd. Be you king also of all those who sit in the ancient superstition of the Gentiles, and refuse not you to deliver them out of darkness into the light and kingdom of God. Grant, O Lord, to your Church, assurance of freedom and immunity from harm; give peace and order to all nations, and make the earth resound from pole to pole with one cry: Praise to the divine heart that wrought our salvation; to it be glory and honor forever. Amen.

FOOTNOTES FROM HAURIETIS AQUAS

1. Is. 12:3.
2. Jas. 1:17.
3. Jn. 7:37-39. (Translator's note: In this passage, Pope Pius XII uses the punctuation favored by St. Irenaeus and St. Cyprian and some other ancient authorities. The translation therefore follows this and not the Douay version.)
4. Cfr. Is. 12:3; Ex. 47:1-12; Zach. 13:1; Ex. 17:1-7; Num. 20:7-13; I Cor. 10:4; Apoc. 7:17, 22:1.
5. Rom. 5:15.
6. I Cor. 6:17.
7. Jn. 4:10.
8. Acts 4:12.
9. Encl. "Annum Sacrum," 25th May, 1899; Acta Leonis, vol. XIX, 1900, pp. 71, 77-79.
10. Pius XI, Encl. "Miserentissimus Redemptor," 8th May, 1928 A.A.S. XX, 1928, p. 167.
11. Cfr. Encl. "Sumni Pontificatus," 20th October, 1939: A.A.S. XXXI, 1939, p. 415.
12. Cfr. A.A.S. XXXII, 1940, p. 170; XXXVII, 1945, pp. 263-264; XL, 1948, p. 501; XLI, 1949, p. 331.
13. Eph. 3:20-21.
14. Is. 12:3.
15. Council Of Ephesus, can. 8; Cfr. Mansi, "Sacrorum Conciliorum Ampliss. Collectio IV," 1083 C.; II Council of Constantinople, can. 9; Cfr. Ibid. IX, 382 E.
16. Cfr. Encl. "Annum Sacrum": Acta Leonis, vol. XIX, 1900, p. 76.
17. Cfr. Ex. 34:27-28.
18. Deut. 6:4-6.
19. St. Thomas, Sum. Theol. II-II, q. 2, a. 7: ed. Leon., vol. VIII, 1895, p. 34.
20. Deut. 32:11.
21. Os. 11:1, 3-4. 14:5-6.
22. Is. 49:14-15.
23. Cant. 2:2, 6:2, 8:6.
24. Jn. 1:14.
25. Jer. 31:3, 31, 33-34.
26. Cfr. Jn. 1:29; 9:18-28, 10:1-17.
27. Jn. 1:16-17.
28. Jn. 21:20.
29. Eph. 3:17-19.
30. Sum. Theol. III, q. 48, a. 2: ed. Leon., vol. XI, 1903, p. 464.
31. Cfr. Encl. "Miserentissimus Redemptor": A.A.S. XX, 1928, p. 170.
32. Eph. 2:4; Sum. Theol. III, q. 46, a. 1 ad 3: ed. Leon., vol. XI, p. 436.
33. Eph. 3:18.
34. Jn. 4:24.
35. 2 Jn. 7.

36. Cfr. Lk. 1:35.
37. St. Leo the Great, Epist. dogm. 'Lectis dilectionis tuae' ad Flavianum Const. Patr., 13 June, a. 449; Cfr. P.L. XIV, 763.
38. Council of Chalcedon, a. 451.
39. Cfr. Mansi, Op. cit., VIII, 115B.
40. Cfr. Sum. Theol. III, q. 15, a. 4; q. 18, a. 6: ed. Leon., vol. X(1) ,1903, pp.189, 237.
41. Cfr. I Cor. 1:23.
42. Heb. 2:11-14, 17-18.
43. Apol. II, 13; P.G. VI, 465.
44. Epist. 261, 3: P.G. XXXII, 972.
45. "In Ioann.", Homil. 63, 2: P.G. LIX, 350.
46. "De fide ad Gratianum," II, 7, 56: P.L. XVI, 594.
47. Cfr. Super Mt. 26:27: P.L. XXVI, 205.
48. Enarr. in Ps. LXXXVII, 3: P. L. XXXVII, 1111.
49. "De Fide Orth.," III, 6 P.G. XCIV, 1006.
50. Ibid. III, 20: P.G. XCIV, 1081.
51. Sum. Theol. I-II, q. 48, a. 4: ed. Leon., vol. VI, 1891, p. 306.
52. Col. 2:9.
53. Cfr. Sum Theol. III, q. 9 aa. 1-3: ed. Leon., vol. XI, 1903, p. 142.
54. Cfr. Ibid. Ill, q. 33, a. 2, ad 3m; q. 46, a: ed. Leon., vol. XI, 1903, pp. 342, 433.
55. Tit. 3:4.
56. Mt. 27:50; Jn. 19:30.
57. Eph. 2:7.
58. Heb. 10:5-7, 10.
59. Registr. epist., lib. IV, ep. 31, ad Theodorum medicum: P.L. LXXVII, 706.
60. Mk. 8:2.
61. Mt. 23:37.
62. Mt. 21:13.
63. Mt. 26:39.
64. Mt. 26:50; Lk. 22-48.
65. Lk. 23:28, 31.
66. Lk. 23:34.
67. Mt. 27:46.
68. Lk. 23:43.
69. Jn. 19:28.
70. Lk. 23:46.
71. Lk. 22:15.
72. Lk. 22:19-20.
73. Mal. 1:11.
74. "De sancta virginitate," VI:P.L. XL, 399.
75. Jn. 15:13.
76. I Jn. 3:16.
77. Gal. 2:20.
78. Cfr. Sum. Theol. III, q. 19, a. 1: ed. Leon., vol. XI, 1903, p. 329.

79. Sum. Theol., Suppl., q. 42, a. 1. ad 3m: ed. Leon., vol. XII, 1906, p. 31.

80. Hymn at Vespers, Feast of the Most Sacred Heart of Jesus.

81. Sum. Theol. III, q. 66, a. 3m: ed. Leon., vol XII, 1906, p. 65.

82. Eph. 5:2.

83. Eph. 4:8, 10.

84. Jn. 14:16.

85. Col. 2:3.

86. Rom. 8:35, 37-39.

87. Eph. 5:25-27.

88. Cfr. 1 Jn. 2:1.

89. Heb. 7:25.

90. Heb. 5:7.

91. Jn. 3:16.

92. St. Bonaventure, Opusc. X: "Vitis mystica," c. III, n. 5; "Opera Omnia," Ad Claras Aquas (Quaracchi) 1898, vol. VIII, p. 164.; Cfr. Sum Theol. III, q. 54, a. 4:ed. Leon., vol. XI, 1903, p. 513.

93. Rom. 8:32.

94. Cfr. Sum. Theol. III, q. 48, a. 5: ed. Leon., vol. XI, 1903, p. 467.

95. Lk. 12:50.

96. Jn. 20:28.

97. Jn. 19:37; Cfr. Zach. 12:10.

98. Cfr. Encl. "Miserentissimus Redemptor": A.A.S. XX, 1928, pp. 167-168.

99. Cfr. A. Gardellini, "Decreta authentica," 1857, n.4579. vol. III, p. 174.

100. Cfr. Decr. S.C. Rit., apud. N. Nilles, "De rationibus festorum Sacratissimi Cordis Jesu et purissimi Cordis Mariae," 5a ed., Innsbruck, 1885, vol. I, p. 167.

101. Eph. 3:14, 16-19.

102. Tit. 3:4.

103. Jn. 3:17.

104. Jn. 4:23-24.

105. Innocent XI, Apostolic Constitution "Coelestis Pater," 19th Nov., 1687; Bullarium Romanum, Rome, 1734, vol. VIII, p. 443.

106. Sum. Theol. II-II, q. 81, a. 3 ad 3m: ed. Leon., vol. IX, 1897, p. 180.

107. Jn. 14:6.

108. Jn. 13:34, 15:12.

109. Jer. 31:31.

110. "Comment, in Evang. S. Ioan.," c. XIII, lect. VII, 3: ed. Parmae, 1860, vol. X, p. 541.

111. Sum. Theol. II-II, q. 82, a. 1: ed. Leon., vol. IX, 1897, p. 187.

112. Ibid. I, q. 38, a. 2: ed. Leon., vol. IV, 1888, p. 393.

113. Mk. 12:30; Mt. 22:37.

114. Cfr. Leo XIII, Encl. "Annum Sacrum: Acta Leonis," vol. XIX, 1900, p. 71 sq; Decree of the Sacred Congregation of Rites, 28th June, 1899, in Decr. Auth. III, n. 3712; Encl. Miserentissimus Redemptor: A.A.S. 1928, p. 177 sq.; Decr. S.C. Rit., 29 Jan. 1929: A.A.S. XXI, 1929, p. 77.

115. Lk. 15:22.

116. Exposit. in Evang. sec. Lucam, 1, X, n. 175: P.L. XV, 1942.

117. Cfr. Sum Theol. II-II, q. 34, a. 2: ed. Leon., vol. VIII, 1895, p. 274.

118. Mt. 24:12.

119. Cfr. Encl. "Miserentissimus Redemptor": A.A.S. XX, 1928, p. 166.

120. Is. 32:17.

121. Encl. "Annum Sacrum: Acta Leonis," vol. XIX, 1900, p. 79; Encl. "Miserentissimus Redemptor": A.A.S. XX, 1928, p. 167.

122. "Litt. Apost. quibus Archisodalitas a Corde Eucharistico Jesu ad S. Ioachim de Urbe erigitur," 17th Feb., 1903; Acta Leonis, vol. XXII, 1903, p. 116.

123. St. Albert the Great, "De Eucharistia," dist. VI, tr. 1., c. 1: Opera Omnia, ed. Borgnet, vol. XXXVIII, Paris, 1890, p. 358.

124. Encl. "Tametsi: Acta Leonis," vol. XX, 1900, p. 303.

125. Cfr. A.A.S. XXXIV, 1942, p. 345 sq.

126. From the Roman Missal, Preface of Christ the King.

Printed in Great Britain
by Amazon

63091701R00051